ADVANCE PRₐ
(CONTINUED FROM THE BACK COVER)

"If you believe data is the new oil, but also realize that turning data into fuel for an omnichannel transformation is not a simple task, then you need to read this book. Stacked with inspirational examples, this book is your toolbox for how to orchestrate tactics and instruments to build a true omnichannel business."

BEREND SIKKENGA
Head of E-commerce at LEGO and
author of textbooks on digital marketing

"*Make It All About Me* is required reading for executives and marketers looking to implement effective growth strategies in the future. Understanding the omnichannel model, addressing the evolution of consumer behaviour, and being able to utilize artificial intelligence are essential elements for attracting and retaining loyal clients. The concepts and guidance in this book come together to provide the instruction manual that will be used to create successful marketing programs going forward."

DAN KLEIN
CEO, Sage Marketing

"It's rare that authors can take the full world of marketing and put it into such tangible advice. Rasmus and Colin do exactly that in *Make It All About Me*. Read as a how-to manual or as a way to focus your efforts and grow your results".

DAVID ANDREADAKIS
Chief Strategy Officer, Kobie Marketing

Published by

LID Publishing Limited

The Record Hall, Studio 204,

16-16a Baldwins Gardens,

London EC1N 7RJ, UK

524 Broadway, 11th Floor, Suite 08-120,

New York, NY 10012, US

info@lidpublishing.com

www.lidpublishing.com

A member of:

BPR
Business Publishers Roundtable

www.businesspublishersroundtable.com

Printed in the Czech Republic by Finidr
ISBN: 978-1-912555-14-7

Cover and page design: Matthew Renaudin

MAKE

RASMUS HOULIND

IT ALL

COLIN SHEARER

ABOUT

LEVERAGING OMNICHANNEL AND AI FOR MARKETING SUCCESS

ME

LID

MADRID | MEXICO CITY | LONDON
NEW YORK | BUENOS AIRES
BOGOTA | SHANGHAI | NEW DELHI

CONTENTS

PREFACE

This book and the Omnichannel Hexagon saw the light of day in 2015 when I first published the Danish book *Hvis det handler om mig, så køber jeg!* At the time of writing it, I was Strategy Director at the digital agency Magnetix and felt there was a need to cut through all the clutter and hype over digital communications, personalization and Big Data. However, I quickly realized that the concept of 'omnichannel' – covering what companies can do to align their efforts to the fact that customers utilize all conceivable communication and sales channels in their interaction with a brand – was too broad a topic for me to tackle alone. So, I started a thorough research process. I invited people from top positions within marketing, digital and data science to participate in roundtable sessions and interviews. Thereafter, I gradually clarified and conceptualized the Omnichannel Hexagon.

Throughout the research process it became clear that there was a clear need for a no-nonsense approach to omnichannel so that people from different departments in an organization could more easily talk about omnichannel without misunderstanding each other. So, when I got the chance to extend the Omnichannel Hexagon maturity model into an online benchmark tool, leveraging knowledge and technology from the Danish Chamber of Commerce and Networked Business Initiative, I clearly felt the beginning of something big. Although I had no idea where it would take me.

The first book reached impressive sales numbers and wide application within Nordic companies and agencies alike.

I received interest as a speaker and a consultant and have to date given more than 100 talks throughout the Nordics and in the UK.

After having seen the model and the online benchmark tool in action and experiencing how people from all over the world and from all parts of organizations responded to the 'simplistic complexity' of the Omnichannel Hexagon, it was clear to me that the model had potential to move beyond the Nordics. And so, I began to alter the model and adjust the book to suit a wider geographical context and more recent times.

A lot has happened since the first book was published in 2015. Back then predictive analytics was something applied by only the largest and most ambitious companies in the Nordics. In 2017, however, we saw the renaissance of AI (artificial intelligence) and it became one of the most-used buzzwords today. Nonetheless it testifies to a new level of maturity within data analytics and more and more organizations have seen the potential for how a structured and ambitious approach with this discipline can deliver transformational benefits.

I first met Colin Shearer in 2016. Colin had graduated in AI when I attended first grade in school and had gone on to found the company that built the market-leading predictive analytics product Clementine, now known as IBM SPSS Modeler. In an impressive career with SPSS and IBM, Colin worked with many major international companies, helping them set their strategy around AI and predictive analytics. Who would be better to have onboard and guide our readers through the marvels of AI?

The foundation for working with data within marketing has also undergone a tremendous change. Ironically, the EU General Data Protection Regulation (GDPR), that has the goal of protecting the consumer, and sets constraints for how organizations can collect and process consumer data, has also made it a lot easier for marketing departments to access and use whatever data made it through the audit processes. GDPR has forced IT departments across all organizations to take control of their customer data and make it available for the consumer and the marketing department alike. Hence the days of marketing departments building shadow-IT environments are gone, and the marketing and the IT departments are collaborating more closely than ever before.

Customer-centricity and omnichannel have also gained more widespread acceptance as profitable business models among both top-level management and senior managers in general. As a consequence, it has become easier to gain top-level backing for initiatives regarding mass personalization across all communication and sales channels. And evangelizing it has become easier than ever; there are more and more cases out there of companies successfully profiting from omnichannel, and a corresponding growth in studies that document the value of the omnichannel approach.

So obviously this book has undergone tremendous changes, and, even though the core of the model still retains more or less its original form, the book has been totally rewritten. The online benchmark tool has also undergone tremendous changes – both in terms of updated questions and in terms of increased contextual help for both answering and interpreting answers to help respondents set a future direction for succeeding with omnichannel and AI within marketing.

I sincerely hope you will find both the book and online benchmark tool useful as well as entertaining.

Rasmus Houlind

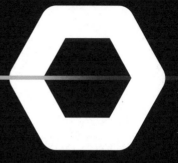

INTRODUCTION
TO THE BOOK

DEBBIE GETS READY FOR THE PARTY

Debbie didn't know what to wear next Saturday for Christine's birthday party. She took out her mobile, opened Instagram and found in her feed a cool look made by one of the new stylists from Nordstrom. It pictured a beautiful girl wearing a skirt, a shirt and a belt. When she clicked the post, she was linked to the products on the Nordstrom website, where she downloaded the app and signed up.

Debbie decided to give the three items from the look a chance so she added them to her wishlist and clicked 'reserve'. She hadn't tried this feature before, so she wasn't sure what to expect. A confirmation note promised her that a sales associate would get the items ready for her within two hours.

Half an hour later she received a notification from Nordstrom that the products were ready for her to try on at her local store. When she approached the store, she received another notification, giving her more precise instructions on where to go to find her reservation. But, when she tried on the items, it was clear to her that she still didn't know what to wear next Saturday.

A few days later she got a notification on the app encouraging her to try out the new 'style boards' that Nordstrom offered. She only had to answer a few questions about her style and preferences so this seemed like less of a commitment than having a real personal shopper. Saturday was approaching, and she had to think of something soon.

Later that day she was notified that her stylist had put together a style board just for her. Viewing it in the app, she was quite impressed. There were definitely some great suggestions. As she already had a skirt that would match the suggested shirt, and since she was familiar with this brand's sizes, she decided to purchase the shirt right away and pick it up immediately. She didn't even have to enter the store – a staff member brought it to her right there in the car while she waited. Now she was ready for Saturday, and she'd definitely be shopping with Nordstrom again!

A FICTIONAL STORY THAT COULD BE TRUE

Debbie's story, as described above, is fictional – but not unfeasible. Nordstrom, being one of the most technically advanced department stores in the world, has already implemented technology[1] that supports all parts of this small narrative. Apart from this, Nordstrom is investing heavily in other parts of its omnichannel strategy – in terms of advanced supply chain optimization, new store formats requiring less real estate space (Nordstrom Local), turning data analytics into personalization at scale and consistently training its employees in using all this technology to 'help customers express their style'. Nordstrom wants to win by combining the best of the physical and the digital areas of shopping, all with the aim of becoming the best fashion retailer. As the title of this book suggests – they're making it all about the customer.

As Nordstrom reported at its investor day[2] in July 2018, customers who engage with Nordstrom's digital features – such as reserve in-store, 'click'n'collect' (also known as BOPIS, or buy online and pick up in-store), style boards and stylists – spend between two and five times as much as the average customer. This tendency is backed up by a *Harvard Business Review* study[3] from 2017 that shows how omnichannel customers spend 4-10% more on their first purchase and place 23% more repeat orders within a year.

On a broader level, the Boston Consulting Group states that leaders within personalization show two to three times faster growth than average companies:

Over the next five years in three sectors alone – retail, health care, and financial services – personalization will push a revenue shift of some $800 billion to the 15% of companies that get it right. [4]

The Boston Consulting Group goes on to describe its view of the path to success:

For incumbents to defend – and expand – share, they need to reimagine their business with an individualized value proposition at the core, merging physical and digital experiences to deepen their customer connections. They need to put brand individualization at the forefront of their strategy agenda to influence everything that they do, including marketing, operations, merchandising, and product development. [5]

Nordstrom is not alone in investing in an omnichannel strategy. A study from the second half of 2017 by Brightpearl, "The State of Omnichannel Retail", states that as many as 91% of the retailers surveyed already had either an omnichannel strategy or a plan to invest in omnichannel, while 87% of them agreed that omnichannel was critical or very important for them. [6] However, only 8% indicated that they had mastered omnichannel. That's what we call a large execution gap!

Retailers are under heavy pressure from international pure-play e-commerce giants such as Amazon.com and Alibaba.com. Amazon is already the biggest player in e-commerce – it is a heavy-hitter in terms of convenience and service. From the East come JD.com and Alibaba.com, with Chinese-government-backed business and goods at a fraction of the price.

Consumers today do not distinguish between e-commerce and commerce. Nor do they care whether they buy from a local company or not – and it is not even certain that they will notice if they haven't. They expect a seamless experience when they switch between digital and physical sales and between communication channels, and they get annoyed when companies send them irrelevant offers that do not take account of the history they have with the company.

Consumers are ready to give up data, and to a certain extent privacy, in favour of convenience and financial benefits. That is where the opportunity lies. Companies will have to seize this opportunity. It starts with building up loyal customer bases, where the companies themselves collect and process data. Companies can then control how the data will be used to create a better, more relevant and welcoming experience for their customers – both on online channels and in the physical store, as well as when customers come to them and when they reach out to the customers.

But this will require a fundamental transformation on the part of businesses: a conversion involving business models, organization and technology. That is what this book is all about.

THIS BOOK ...

... is a suggestion of how to leverage omnichannel and AI (artificial intelligence) for marketing and business success. We believe that the chief marketing officer is well equipped for leading organizations in the omnichannel transformation that is needed. Marketing and business success therefore go hand in hand.

On the basis of our experience in this field, input from more than 100 specialists within the industry, and the latest articles and literature, we have developed the Omnichannel Hexagon as a model for gauging omnichannel maturity. The hexagon provides a framework for targeting your marketing efforts and ensuring that every step you take is a step closer to continuously improving the customer experience without sacrificing profitability.

This book will present the six disciplines to master and how to manage them in a more customer-centric manner. You will get an overview of how far along your organization is in working with omnichannel, and what barriers might impede your further progress in it.

You can match your company with the four archetypal types of omnichannel maturity and find help with formulating a strategy for furthering the process. In addition, the model will serve as a litmus test of whether and how you should organize your next project, and which factors you should take into account to really bring you closer to the best possible and most profitable customer experience.

Each chapter in this book corresponds to one of the six disciplines in the Omnichannel Hexagon, introducing central themes for the discipline being discussed. The goal is to provide insights into the relationships between the themes and disciplines, and the optimal, most profitable customer experience.

To help demystify omnichannel marketing, each chapter opens with an example that focuses on the discipline in question. These narratives are fictional stories inspired by both articles and dialogue with the companies depicted – they are by no means intended to be accurate representations of reality but merely sources of inspiration.

A similar disclaimer is important to make with regards to legal topics that we are touching upon in the book. The tactics mentioned are by no means guaranteed to be considered legal by all worldwide legislations. Consult a legal advisor with expertise in local legislation before you do anything too hasty.

We wish you a profitable reading experience.

Rasmus Houlind and Colin Shearer,
June 2019

TOWARDS AN OMNICHANNEL TRANSFORMATION

In the business world today, we are seeing companies moving on from the initial hype and enthusiasm for new technology and communication channels to a place where they can start to apply these powerful technologies and communication channels with a razor-sharp focus on winning more customers and keeping them profitable.

To put it briefly, we are seeing more and more companies moving from a sales-oriented multichannel focus to an omnichannel focus where customer profitability and customer loyalty are at the heart of all major decisions. There is more on those topics below.

Digital hype and excitement

Needless to say, the advent of digital brought tremendous initial excitement. Marketers suddenly had an ever-increasing array of new communication channels and digital tools at their disposal. The first questions were naturally around how all of these new tools worked. What could marketers now achieve? How could they better accomplish the goals that they were already working towards?

From multichannel to omnichannel

Within marketing this led to multichannel marketing, which is the ability to use multiple communication channels in marketing and sales. Seen from a contemporary standpoint, there was a tendency for marketing functions to copy traditional marketing mechanisms over to the – at that time – new digital channels. As an end customer you would meet the same campaign everywhere – but it wouldn't take into account the totality of your personal history with each company.

In pure multichannel marketing, data can be collected and used within each channel to at most suboptimize the performance for precisely that channel. There are no incentives for anything else, at least not for the individual employee. Multichannel focuses on the individual communication channels, which can be great for building a really good app or a website. But, when it comes to integrating the channels, challenges arise.

Cross-channel marketing is the stepping stone between multichannel and omnichannel. The fundamental difference between multi- and cross-channel marketing lies in the use of data. In cross-channel marketing, there is a recognition that the customer will switch channels many times on a purchasing journey. Channel managers are encouraged to obtain data from other channels, since broader data will create better results for personalization and segmentation. But at this stage the customer-centric organization is not yet in place, so silos are still strong, with internal rivalry and suboptimizing of 'non-customer-centric' objectives, tools and data silos.

Omnichannel is the next level of marketing, where the entire organization has accustomed itself to the fact that customers' buying decisions are not linear. In principle, every communication channel is bidirectional and data is gathered and stored by organizations for use in later interactions via all other communication channels – hence the prefix 'omni'. In practice, the customer service centre knows immediately if the customer it has on the line is one who opens their email and has recently been logged in; it also knows what the customer has previously purchased, both online and in-store. There is no channel conflict, and the employees are not biased to push the customer in a particular direction but are able to help the customer on the purchasing journey in an open and well-informed way. All outbound communications are also tailored on the basis of customers' previous interactions with the company, as well as their stated or deduced interests and preferences. All together this maximizes the relevance for each customer – and thus gets them to buy earlier, more and more often, and to tell their friends about their positive experience.

SINGLE CHANNEL

MULTICHANNEL

CROSS-CHANNEL

OMNICHANNEL

As the description of omnichannel above clearly indicates, omnichannel success takes a more profound effort from the whole organization and entails moving far beyond simply 'going digital'.

Throughout this book, we will refer to both sales and communication channels simply as 'channels'. When we refer to 'omnichannel marketing', we will be referring specifically to the discipline of personalizing customer communication across all channels, whereas when we refer to 'omnichannel' in general, it will cover both omnichannel marketing and omnichannel commerce.

Omnichannel is for all industries

Even though retailers and consumer-based retail brands have been quick to embrace omnichannel as a concept, the term is by no means exclusive to these types of business. Just because a certain business doesn't have physical products or stores doesn't mean that customers limit themselves to one single communication or sales channel in their search, or when they are looking for after-sales service. Getting omnichannel right as a retail business requires a lot of supply chain and inventory management – something that other industries may not need to do. To make this book widely applicable, we have deliberately chosen not to cover the entire supply chain discussion but instead focus on the communication and data aspects.

Beyond a digital transformation

Exploring new tools and how digital could enhance all kinds of functions within enterprises led to heavy debate around digital transformation. How should companies embrace digital technology to support existing business processes and to innovate and invent new business models?

The odds are that by now:

- Your organization has an established presence in relevant digital and social channels.
- You are on your third-generation (or Nth-generation) website.
- You are doing email marketing.
- You have experimented with personalization in most communication channels.
- You are using ad-spend on programmatic advertising.
- You are thinking about digital in the way you develop your products and services.
- You are using business intelligence to provide numbers and forecasts as well as support procurement.

So, although things could potentially continue in this way, and you haven't yet exhaustively explored what all technology can do for every part of your business, it's already time to refocus and enter into what we call an omnichannel transformation.

Customer expectations call for an omnichannel transformation

Another significant business trend that stresses the need for an omnichannel transformation can be summed up as 'the Age of the Customer'[7] or 'B2Me'[8]. At its core, this is all about putting the customers and their expectations of individual treatment first, reaching them with a relevant product or a personalized message, and doing so at precisely the right time.

The idea of accommodating customer needs on a one-to-one basis is nothing new. In 1993, authors Don Peppers and Martha Rogers wrote their book *The One-to-One Future*, which has since then become famous for its foresight.[9] Their point was that it was about time that companies started to define themselves as customer-centric instead of being obsessed with the silos of sales channels and products. "Why now?" you might ask.

According to Jim Blasingame, the author of *The Age of the Customer*[10], since 2015 the digital revolution has led to a game-changing shift in the control of the buying process. The power has shifted towards the consumer since product availability is abundant, the next vendor is never too far away on the internet, all content regarding a product is available in a multitude of places and so are other customers' opinions about this product. Furthermore, it's extremely easy to share both positive and negative experiences and opinions for future customers to see.

This forces businesses to refocus on the customer instead of on their sales channels or on the infinite number of vendors out there promising gold will rain down from the sky if only customers buy their new product.

The digital revolution has brought with it the temptation of a vast array of opportunities. It's time to refocus and make sure that marketers are looking in the right direction, namely towards the customer – all the while applying technology and business insights to help stay on course.

The omnichannel transformation

The transformation into the new omnichannel paradigm implies a profound change within not only marketing but also many other parts of the business.

CEOs need to support and play a central role in changing existing ways of working, not only within marketing and sales but also within data analytics, retail and even HR.

And, even if throughout the organization things are in place for omnichannel marketing, you won't be able to make all communication relevant to everybody all the time. You will never get to a point where you have a complete customer database; you will never have enough data on all your customers, nor all the content you need to always be relevant to everyone. This means that you can't suddenly abandon your one-size-fits-all campaigns. They have to live on.

For most companies, an omnichannel transformation means rebuilding the aircraft while flying it. And, if you aren't given any extra resources, it will be the same people flying the aircraft as those who are rebuilding it.

But in time your entire organization will become customer-centric. It will have a large known customer base, numerous AI models, and vast amounts of content and automated communications going out to the right customers at the right time. Your in-store personnel and customer service agents will be trained and equipped with tools that bridge the gaps between sales and communication channels alike so that customers – for the most part – are met with relevant communication.

That's when the transformation will be complete.

A tool for the marketer

This book is a tool for you, the marketer, to help you steer your organization into a new omnichannel world. To make this tool as comprehensible as possible, we've created the Omnichannel Hexagon as a maturity model to guide you through the transformation. Read on to learn more.

THE OMNICHANNEL HEXAGON

The Omnichannel Hexagon is the main model used in this book. It is a concentration of all the features that span communication and sales channels alike and thus need to be addressed in order to succeed with omnichannel marketing. Since the model is flavoured by neither communication-channel-specific nor department-specific lingo, it provides a neutral language within which you and your colleagues can discuss omnichannel important topics.

The objective of the Omnichannel Hexagon

The objective of the Omnichannel Hexagon is to provide a method to address and assess progress with omnichannel. It will provide your business with a better overview of your journey to omnichannel marketing and what your priorities should be. By mapping your company's position on the model and comparing it with your competitors', it will be apparent where your primary efforts are needed and in which direction you should be moving.

The Omnichannel Hexagon can also help you to secure appropriate resources and the necessary budget from top management. It can be used in management workshops in which different parts of the organization indicate their view on the progress to omnichannel. Talking about the Omnichannel Hexagon and the related disciplines stimulates a change of attitude that will make it easier to work towards omnichannel as a common goal. Read more about this in Chapter 6.

The six disciplines

In order to conduct omnichannel marketing effectively and efficiently, there are six disciplines that you and your business should cultivate to an ever more customer-oriented and sophisticated degree. The disciplines are as follows:

- **Customer recognition and permissions**: The more customers you can recognize across channels and reach out to on your own initiative, the greater the total impact and profitability through personalization you will have, and the less expenditure for exposure on paid media.
- **Data collection**: Data is your company's memory of every single customer and the prerequisite for becoming more relevant in your communication and service. Customer data must be collected systematically and integrated to provide a comprehensive picture of each customer.
- **Data analytics and AI**: Artificial intelligence and predictive analytics provide granular insight into correlations between data and desirable and undesirable customer behaviour. This insight constitutes the treatment of each individual customer as well as the prioritization and estimation of the impact of new omnichannel efforts.
- **Communication and service**: Data and insights are worth nothing, if they aren't being used. Leverage insights from data analytics to develop and deliver the right communication and service to each individual customer at the right time in the right channel. By doing so you acknowledge your history with each customer, both when you turn to your customers and when they come to you.
- **Performance analysis**: If you want to develop a customer-centric organization and measure its success, then you need to monitor metrics that you are not used to. You should incorporate customer metrics in your performance analysis and not just focus on individual channels and campaigns.
- **Organizing and management**: Organization and incentive structures should support optimal customer servicing across channels. Otherwise, individual agendas and targets will quickly block your way to omnichannel. Your business must also possess the right culture, skills and tools.

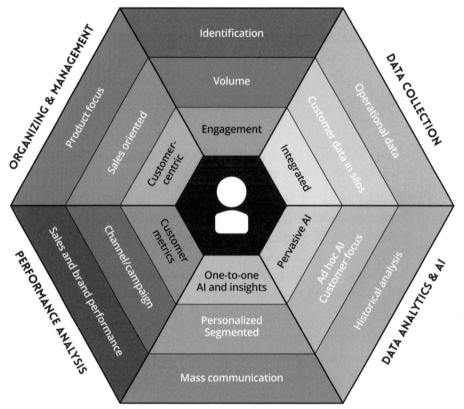

These six disciplines are applicable across all channels. For example, when you assess your company's maturity in Communication & Service, the questions and the answers are relevant for all channels. Maturity is measured from the outside in, understood in the sense that you need to start with assessing whether your business meets the criteria in the outermost ring and then move one level inward towards the centre. Most companies will, at minimum, be in the outermost ring for each discipline.

The disciplines have no fixed order, but in many cases it will be difficult to fully master one discipline without having a certain maturity in another. For example, it makes little sense to do Data Analytics & AI without being fairly sophisticated in Data Collection. It is also difficult to be really relevant in your communication without being able to recognize the customer and have a certain amount of data. The goal is to move slowly inwards across the disciplines, while the interplay among channels and organizational entities is created, preserved and strengthened.

Why is the product not included in the Omnichannel Hexagon?

We've been asked a number of times why the product is not included as a separate discipline in the Omnichannel Hexagon. There are several reasons for this.

First, there are differences in how centred a company is around a single product or a single joint service. Some companies will indeed have one core service that their business will be built around, while others will have many products. In the latter case, it will be more about selecting the right products for each customer than developing the product itself.

Second, some of our readers do not have the opportunity to change the product or service itself to any significant extent. Therefore, having a separate discipline for the product would not be relevant to all.

However, the six disciplines can be used to develop products. For instance, companies should be using the Data Collection and Data Analytics & AI disciplines to better understand their customers and gain insight into their needs.

Communication and service are a big part of the product experience

It is a fact that the perceived value of a product can be significantly affected by the Communication & Service discipline. For example, a customer sees a ring in a shop. The ring has some natural value in that it is beautiful and made of quality materials. But the perceived value can be enhanced if the customer is presented with communication that supports a narrative about the ring, the designer's thoughts on the piece, its artisanal qualities, etc. This provides a better (and perhaps different) experience of the product's value and increases the impact of word-of-mouth and storytelling about the brand. The product, or at least the product experience, is to some extent contained in the Communication & Service discipline.

Why is the brand not included in the Omnichannel Hexagon?

The Omnichannel Hexagon and omnichannel marketing in general will be pointless to employ if the starting point, i.e. the brand, service or price point, is not attractive in itself. The Omnichannel Hexagon takes for granted that your brand understands or speaks to the right emotional values that create an interest and are relevant to your customers. Omnichannel is primarily an enabler, i.e. a way to perform better on an already known and functioning foundation. That is why the brand is not included as a discipline in the model.

However, good execution of omnichannel can greatly impact perception of the brand. Customers will adopt a more positive view of your brand when they learn that your company does not forget their history as they switch from one communication channel to another and when they are consistently met with relevant and timely communication, whether they are interacting with the brand in the physical store or through one of the many digital channels.

The four omnichannel archetypes

Since 2015, when Rasmus Houlind launched the first version of the Omnichannel Hexagon, more than 800 companies have used the original online benchmark tool to assess their omnichannel maturity.

During the data-investigation process, together with the Networked Business Initiative (NBI) and Copenhagen-based PhD in Maturity Models, Lester Lasrado, it became clear that maturity within certain disciplines correlated to a significant degree. This led us to define the following archetypes within omnichannel maturity. The archetypes can help to describe certain states but, more importantly, they set a direction towards omnichannel success, which is where the company takes on the role of a trusted advisor in the eyes of customers.

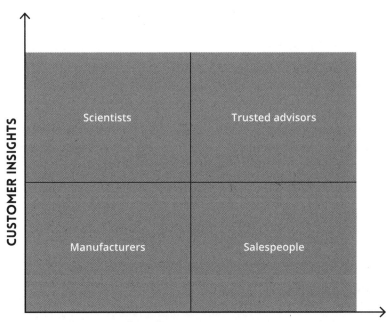

On the X-axis, you can execute direct communication towards customers across communication channels. Companies that excel on this axis are the ones who are fairly mature in the two disciplines of Customer Recognition & Permissions and Communication & Service.

On the Y-axis, you have the degree to which an organization can derive insights from customer behaviour. Companies that excel on the Y-axis are fairly mature in Data Collection and Data Analytics & AI.

The top-right corner represents organizations that are good at communicating directly with customers across channels based on customer insights. In general, it is not possible to achieve the top-right position in the matrix without also being mature in the two disciplines of Organizing & Management and Performance Analysis.

The Manufacturers

Companies that fit the Manufacturer archetype have indirect communications with their end customers and don't record much of their data. Maturity within the Omnichannel Hexagon will generally be low for such companies across all six disciplines. In this archetype we find product-oriented companies that resell their products without ever meeting the end customer one to one. Evolving from this archetype requires a tremendous transformation on all levels. Connections with end customers need to be established if the company wishes to become omnichannel to any degree.

The Scientists

Companies that fit the Scientist archetype generally score well in both Data Collection and Data Analytics & AI, but poorly in Customer Recognition & Permissions and Communication & Service. While these companies do not use analytics to improve communications to and servicing of customers, they do employ insights derived from research and development analytics to improve their core product. These companies tend to be very technologically driven and are often seen building hardware products. For these companies to become more omnichannel, their marketing teams need to take advantage of all the wonderful data that is at their disposal – proactively turning average customer experiences into delightful ones.

The Salespeople

Companies within this archetype generally score well in Customer Recognition & Permissions and Communication & Service, but poorly in Data Collection and Data Analytics & AI. While permission and consent may have been gathered, this will primarily have been done for the purpose of moving from paid media advertising into owned media such as email-, web-, app- and SMS-based communications.[11] This means that there will be no changes made to the traditional one-size-fits-all communications other than the occasional segmentation and personalization of newsletters. In this category you find most traditional retailers which tend to struggle with implementing an omnichannel strategy. Customers often perceive these organizations as salesy and perhaps even pushy. To become more omnichannel, they need to take both data collection and analytics more seriously. This can be achieved if the marketing team begins to incorporate marketing (data) analytics and inspire the organization to adopt data practices to a wider extent.

The Trusted Advisors

In the top-right corner of the model we find the Trusted Advisors. This is where we find the top performers within omnichannel. Companies that fit this archetype excel not only within the four data- and communication-related disciplines but also within Performance Analysis and

Organizing & Management. This archetype proves the point that a company cannot become fully omnichannel without working intensely to adjust its organization and its way of looking at performance analysis towards customer-centricity.

Use the online benchmark tool to assess your company's maturity

Some CEOs are so concerned with their immediate competitors that they neglect to consider whether bigger players such as JD.com or Amazon are going to win the entire market. Therefore, an indication of whether your business is in front of or behind your competitors can be helpful.

For this purpose, we have allied with the NBI. Using the Omnichannel Hexagon, we have jointly developed a new omnichannel benchmark tool that can be used to measure omnichannel maturity. By following the link in the QR code below, you can quickly determine your maturity level within the six disciplines and see where you rank against your competitors.

You can take the survey at this link:

OMNICHANNELFORBUSINESS.ORG

Initially, you will get a chart of your company's maturity that can be used internally. You will be able to narrow down the comparison with your own or similar industries and see how other companies have generally answered the specific questions.

Later you can choose to invite members of your organization to answer the same questions to reveal a more deeply rooted image. It will also be clear where you and your colleagues have different perceptions of things. This can inspire knowledge-sharing and collaboration.

All responses feed into the body of data that NBI gathers for its global study of omnichannel maturity. Your data is private and processed anonymously for inclusion in the benchmark for other companies as well as general analyses.

Apart from an initial benchmark on the Omnichannel Hexagon, the tool also provides you with insights into which archetype your business resembles the most and how this compares with the other respondents.

CUSTOMER RECOGNITION & PERMISSIONS

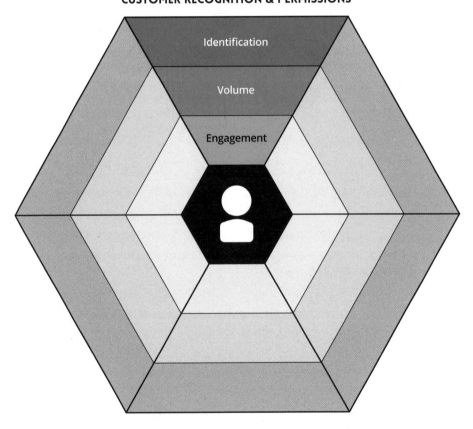

1

CUSTOMER RECOGNITION & PERMISSIONS

Recognizing a customer is the foundation of being personal. How many of your customers can you recognize across channels? And do you have the option of reaching out to them on a one-to-one basis?

Wang Lei lives in Shanghai and his two-year anniversary with his partner Zhang Min is approaching. Wang has never bought jewellery before, but lately he has noticed that his idol Timmy Xu is sharing pictures of himself wearing jewellery from the brand Forevermark on WeChat. Wang clicks the link to the Forevermark WeChat store, follows the brand and adds some necklaces and rings to his wishlist. He's prompted to come and see the products physically in the shop Libert'aime in Shanghai and is able to book an appointment through WeChat.

When Wang Lei gets to the store, he sees people trying on jewellery in front of a 'magic mirror' that takes your picture to share on WeChat so that you can get your friends' opinions on the jewellery before buying. To use it, you have to sign into your WeChat account and enrol in the brand's loyalty programme. Wang finds his details on WeChat and a sales ambassador shows him the products from his wishlist.

Later, Zhang Min is surprised and happy when she unwraps the necklace Wang chose. Occasionally Wang gets notifications from Forevermark and is reminded to shop there in the future.[12]

The example above is a realistic (yet fictitious) scenario of how a customer journey could take place in the Libert'aime store in Shanghai and how Forevermark takes great care to recognize the customer across both communication and sales channels and also asks for consent for later direct communication. It is a great example of exactly what this chapter is about.

We suggest that you learn from how Forevermark combines influencer marketing and social media to reach its potential audience and then uses the WeChat app and e-commerce store to encourage them to connect and identify themselves. Be inspired by how Forevermark uses technology in the store, where customers are recognized, and the shopping experience can continue where it left off on digital channels. This will help you create long-lasting connections between your brand and your customers.

Using the same principles (but, where relevant, perhaps through channels more heavily adopted in your market than WeChat), we suggest that you connect with your customers. To make customers feel that they are at the centre of your attention, you have to be able to recognize them no matter which communication channel you meet them on. You also want the opportunity to be the one who starts the dialogue. Otherwise, it soon becomes a very one-sided relationship. That's why your aim should be to get their consent, also known as permission.

When we talk about customer recognition and permission gathering as the same discipline, it is because there is commonly an overlap between the way you recognize the customer and the way you reach out to the customer. Very often, it is the email address, phone number or app ID (or more than one of these) that is the key to recognizing your customers.

At the same time, they are among the direct communication channels you can have to your customers.

On a more general level, this discipline refers to the necessity of building a large, dedicated base of both customers and non-customers in order to succeed with omnichannel. You must be able to recognize customers across channels no matter whether they enter your stores or call you on the phone. At the same time, you must have the possibility of reaching out to customers when you have something on your mind that you wish to take action upon – preferably tailoring this message using the data you have for each and every customer.

Systematic customer recognition and permission gathering is the first of the six disciplines in the Omnichannel Hexagon. It is the foundation for personalizing your communication and the key to being able to analyse data going forward. If you don't know who you are talking to, how will you be able to 'make it all about them'?

Moving on to the permission part – you cannot always count on customers seeking you out. "Build it and they will come!" is perhaps true if you have the most amazing product in the world or the craziest budget for content marketing. But who has that?

If your customers are to feel that you have a bidirectional relationship, then you must be able to recognize them across all channels. Your brand should also take the initiative once in a while – although not all the time and not too aggressively, otherwise individuals will feel pressured and 'sold to' rather than invested in as loyal customers.

PROFITABILITY LIES IN SCALING REACH ON OWNED MEDIA

It is expensive constantly having to buy your own customers' attention on Google or Facebook, not to mention TV, print or radio. As a category these communication channels are referred to as 'paid media'. Once you have paid Google to reel in a customer who has perhaps already searched for your brand name, it feels quite ridiculous having to pay again so that the same customer will also click on your Google ad next time.

Owned media is a term covering all the communication channels where you don't have to pay someone else for the exposure. So in practice this accounts for (at least) email, web, app, SMS and even the physical signage within or on your brick-and-mortar stores. The sooner you start moving the dialogue from paid into owned media, the better (and cheaper).

Any self-respecting retail brand today has some form of loyalty programme with an associated marketing permission. But, more often than not, permission gathering is seen as a pure digital activity and club membership may not even be recognized in the physical store at all. This is despite the fact that this can easily become the best-performing source for new club members – and, equally importantly, behavioural data. There is more about these 'channel conflicts' in Chapter 6.

Scale puts 'meat' on the segments

Another significant benefit of having built up a large customer and permission base is that as the database grows, so does the size of the underlying segments into which it makes sense to divide the database.

Quite practically, we know that personalizing the content and timing of a given push communication can dramatically increase its impact – by as much as 200% to even 900%.[13] However, if the actual number of customers that will be reached by personalized communication is low – as it will be before critical mass is obtained – this can mean that the additional cost of preparing the personalized content will not pay for itself. A high permission volume will mean more meat on even the smaller segments of your customer database and make it much more profitable to develop and send personalized content for them.

If your business adopts automated communication (trigger communication, marketing automation, etc.), a large permission base will also provide a greater volume of automated communication going out to relevant targets on a regular basis. This communication can have a very high degree of efficiency and it costs only marginally more to reach a much wider audience.

Club membership as the hero in the ad

Traditional paid media, such as TV commercials, has the advantage that it can often scale very rapidly. If you have a message today that you would like to see cause an effect very quickly, mass marketing can still do something quite unique. Despite the trend of watching programmes on online streaming services, there are still a great many households that watch traditional TV channels every evening. If your advertisements run today, there will be increased demand for your product tomorrow and there will be a higher chance of you reaching your quarterly budget. If you have to gather permissions first, then sales won't come until you market to that permission base. So, do you have the luxury of thinking and acting long term?

More and more traditional ads are ending with an announcement that one can enrol in some form of loyalty programme or news service, or download an app, which then immediately gives the end customer a sales-oriented promotion. In this way, companies can achieve both the short-term and the long-term result.

WORKING WITH CUSTOMER RECOGNITION AND PERMISSION GATHERING

Very often customers can be identified by their email address. Permissions may be directly equated with email permissions. Historically, authorization to send directly into people's electronic inbox has also been the most frequently used method of direct digital communication. Email is effective, visual and inexpensive to send. Email is still the largest and most efficient channel for your external communication on owned media. That said, there has definitely been a proliferation of the number of channels in use by consumers today. Apart from endless social media options, such as Snapchat, Instagram, Facebook Messenger, not forgetting WeChat in China, it's definitely also worth mentioning text messaging and app push notifications.

In line with the Omnichannel Hexagon and customer-centricity, you can classify permissions according to how close they come to the customer. Can we automatically recognize customers and personalize the message when they show up on our website or in the store on their own initiative? Or can we make a relevant message vibrate right down in their pockets at a relevant time?

It is one thing for a company to recognize customers in each channel independently, but it is another thing to identify each individual customer across channels. You need to be able to link email addresses to phone numbers to make sure you know who you are talking to. The same is true for postal addresses, Facebook profiles and other more unconventional ways of recognizing customers.

Maturity in customer recognition and permission gathering is a matter of both identifying and being able to interconnect different types of permission for the same customer. This must be done for as many customers as possible and on as many channels as possible. Subsequently, it is a matter of keeping them engaged, so they are not just dead meat in the database.

In this chapter we will first review the methods of customer identification across channels and then examine the different types of permission. Then we will go into how to effectively gather permissions via both your own and paid media. Finally, we will discuss maturity within the discipline.

IDENTIFICATION AND RECOGNITION

If it is your intention for your customers to receive personalized messages, then as a minimum you have to be able to recognize them. There are many ways to do this, and some are specific to the channel in question.

Cookies – recognition on the same device

The simplest way of recognizing a customer on a website is by the company placing a small unique file called a 'cookie' on the customer's phone, tablet or computer. This tracks the device so it is recognized if it accesses the website again. It is not a bullet-proof method of tracking individual users, since it is of course possible to imagine that multiple users might use the same tablet, computer or even phone, particularly in the case of shared devices at home or in a library, airport or another public place. Also, it's worth noting that cookies expire after some time, leaving the trail cold.

Ever since the EU Cookie Directive was approved in March 2011, users in Europe have had to actively be made aware that a website is going to install a cookie. However, not all websites have adopted this and most users perceive it as a nuisance having to click 'I accept cookies' when visiting a website for the first time. In May 2018, the GDPR (General Data Protection Regulation) legislation was put into effect in the EU, and the rules have become even more strict. Websites are now required to give users the option of saying no to different types of cookies, and there are increased fines for overstepping these guidelines. At the time of writing, we have yet to see any finished lawsuits with substantial fines for companies not living up to these guidelines. We suppose it's just a matter of time, though.

Despite these and other legal hurdles, it is important to remember that people are no longer surprised when they are recognized by a website; quite the contrary – it is now expected and desired by more and more people.

Login and profile – recognition across devices

If you need a little more certainty that it is the same customer/user who is looking at your website, a login on the site is the best option. However, there must be a good reason for creating such a login for the user – otherwise this option is typically not used. We see this most frequently while completing online purchases, where users are offered the possibility of creating a login to make subsequent purchases easier. The merchant will then save the customer's contact, billing and shipping information, and it will be easier to transact a second time. It makes good sense, if the customer can imagine doing business in the same place again.

Other kinds of functionality may also require a login. One example is the wishlist function, to enable users and potential customers to save products that they might be interested in buying at a later stage. Customers who would like to use this function will be asked to create a login. The website will then remember what is on the customer's wishlist and there will be no need to log in again later on this device – unless the customer actively logs out. It is considered a service for the customer to be able to save products of particular interest, especially when the product assortment is overwhelming.

An added benefit for the company is that they can now recognize this individual again – both later on the same machine and on other devices – as long as the individual logs in using their profile. In addition, the company will gain valuable knowledge from the contents of the wishlist and may even manage to tempt the customer with a discount voucher in exchange for agreeing to receive offers and newsletters.

Bait for email, name and title

If a strong incentive is not immediately provided for the user to create a profile, you can use a known tactic from B2B (business-to-business) lead generation. Companies offer free downloads of white papers and e-books in exchange for users giving their name, title and email address. Regardless of whether the user checks the box to receive marketing materials, you can now with 95% accuracy attribute the page and product views from this device to a concrete prospect, whom you can then contact in other ways. Of course, this requires a CMS (content management system) that supports this function, or installation of a proper tracking tool on the site.

For instance, you don't have to download many white papers from Sitecore.net before it knows whether you are interested in a demo of its software – which, incidentally, is the very same software Sitecore uses to collect this data. Sitecore is not the only CMS that supports this; there are a number of similar tools.

Recognition in the physical store

In the old days, it was no big deal to recognize customers who often came into a store. The owners, who were often standing behind the counter themselves, got a feeling for which customers visited their store frequently. A talented sales associate would nod familiarly at returning customers and maybe even remember their sizes and their previous purchases.

Although this still occurs, the retail trade today is characterized by ever-larger stores with often less experienced sales associates and a high turnover of these employees. And, when international chains are spread across multiple locations, cities and countries, it is in practice impossible to recognize customers from branch to branch without some kind of common identifier. The solution for physical retail is very often a loyalty programme.

Customer recognition via a loyalty programme

In order to recognize customers, retailers set up loyalty programmes. In exchange for providing information about themselves and identifying themselves when making a purchase, customers receive some type of advantage in the form of discounts, other services or privileges, such as invitations to special sales and events.

One of the problems for most clubs, unfortunately, is that it is only at checkout (the point of sale, or POS) that customers identify themselves. Therefore, it is usually not possible for the sales associate to provide the same personal guidance and service to the customer that would have been possible if they had been recognized in the old-fashioned physical way. Personalized assistance can only be given when the customer has already made a purchase decision and stood in line at the register – and that is often too late.

The phone is the key to in-store customer recognition

Long gone are the days when loyalty programme membership equalled carrying around yet another plastic card in your wallet. Membership cards have now moved into customers' mobile phones in the form of apps.

Besides relieving customers from dragging along extra plastic cards, mobile apps have the advantage of supporting so-called 'geo fencing' using beacon technology, Wi-Fi or GPS. These methods all have more or less the same effect. As soon as a customer (who has given their consent in the app) enters a certain geographical area, something happens. For example, the customer could get a promotional message, but, more importantly, the retailer will now know that this customer is nearby or even in-store. This will help in terms of data collection and also mean the sales associates can be notified. This was in effect what we saw in the opening of this chapter with the Forevermark example.

Over the past few years many grocery chains have deployed self-service checkouts where customers first use an app to scan a barcode in-store to let the store know they are there and then scan products as they add them to their shopping basket. With a credit card registered in the app, this makes checkout so much easier. This is, for instance, the case with Waitrose's Quick Check and Selfridges' Scan & Go.

As addressed in more detail in the next chapter – Data Collection – the added advantage for the store is that purchases are no longer anonymous. In this way, knowledge about purchases in physical stores can be used in future digital communications with customers. Additionally, this helps to inform all channels of the service the customer previously experienced when they were recognized by the shop staff.

Companies that are good at recognizing customers in-store have a head start in omnichannel. Nordstrom (a North American chain of department stores) has around 50% of its purchases registered with members of its loyalty programme,[14] whereas according to the National Retail Federation, Williams Sonoma brands can, due to the company's mail-order heritage, connect a name, email address and physical address to 70% of purchases.[15] As we shall see in the opening of Chapter 2, Amazon Go has taken this to a whole new level. It simply doesn't allow anonymous visitors into its stores.

Voice recognition in the customer centre

Voice recognition is no longer science fiction. Not to be confused with speech recognition, which can determine *what* is being said, voice recognition can determine a speaker's identity through biometrics. This can greatly reduce call centre operation speed. Each customer profile will have a voice 'footprint' – in other words, a registration of each customer's sound.[16]

Facial recognition

China is one of the most pioneering countries in terms of exploring new technologies (and, it is also worth mentioning, the country is less concerned with privacy issues than the EU). It has already enabled facial recognition in Shanghai Airport, making it extremely easy for Chinese citizens to check in.[17] The plan is to also implement this in Shanghai Metro, coupled with speech recognition and digital payment provider Alipay. Commuters will simply need to look into the camera and say out loud where they intend to go and they will automatically be let in and their account will be charged.[18]

TYPES OF PERMISSION – INITIATIVE FOR COMMUNICATION

There is a big difference between just being able to recognize customers and having the right to occasionally initiate dialogue with them. It is important to have consent to send information and offers to each individual customer without the customer prompting this communication. This is backed by a study conducted by the media agency OMD and Insights Group showing that 75% of the market for your product consists of passive customers who will only take action if you or your competitors reach out.[19] The more customers that can be recognized and contacted (with permission), the more profitable customer relationships you will have. In the following sections, we will review the different types of permission and related topics.

Social media is paid media

If you can get your customers to follow your brand page or profile on websites such as Twitter or Facebook, in theory you will have some of your posts appear in their newsfeed, which they will likely check once in a while. Instead of relying on your customers coming by your website or store, you will now have the possibility of reaching them more directly.

However, there is no guarantee that your prospects will check their Facebook or Twitter newsfeed. Furthermore, social media sites are increasingly having to capitalize on their business customers, with the result that you as a business owner must again pay to boost the visibility of your message to your followers.

If you choose to pay for increased exposure on Facebook, there is then the possibility of segmenting your editorial message by gender, age, education, geography, language, marital status and interests. If you import specific lists of people (names, emails and phone numbers) to Facebook that you know share certain behaviour (i.e. have purchased the same product), you can be fairly sure you are reaching the right people. However, there is no guarantee that you are totally right and there is no possibility of merging each customer's name, purchase history or external data into your messaging.

The point is that you never really get close to customers on social media without it being really expensive or manual. So, this social permission is therefore not the most profitable one, but it can still be valuable to have a large number of followers on social media. If the content that you choose to share is fun and interesting, it can lead to great exposure, especially if your followers are commenting on and sharing it. Bear in mind, though, that posts carrying a very sales-oriented message (e.g. a discount) tend not to get commented on or shared.

Postal address and direct mail

You can also consider the physical address as a possibility for communicating directly to customers. If your customers are not registered on lists prohibiting them from receiving offers through the mail, you may write physical letters to them. You should check each address against a country's 'Robinson list', which is a public list of the names and associated addresses of people who have opted out of receiving direct marketing in their mailbox.

Postal mailings are the traditional channel for direct marketing. With the use of advanced merge rules, potentially augmented by AI, you have the freedom to create the right personal message and deliver it directly into the recipient's address. But this is not very cost-effective. If you choose to send direct marketing to your customers, you should consider design, printing, packing and postage costs. Direct mail can easily amount to over €3.00 per piece for printing, packing and postage alone.

Although postal delivery is relatively expensive, it does have its advantages. The opening rate is typically very high. Today customers rarely get letters in their physical mailbox so when they suddenly do, they almost always open them. The DMA (Data & Marketing Association) in the US claims that the response rates for direct mail tend to be anywhere between 10 and 30 times higher than for email.[20]

Postal addresses have the added advantage that to a large extent they can be purchased in bulk.[21] It is even possible to buy them segmented by household statistical data such as presumed media habits, political attitudes and income. Therefore, if you find yourself having to create new customer relationships and you have a target group that is unevenly distributed in other media groups, this can be a fine media choice.

Email permission

Win a €300 gift card! Sign up for our newsletter!

You've probably seen this message many times – in several variants, of course. Retailers of all sizes today have email lists and newsletters. Email is still the most cost-effective outbound communication channel, with the capability of being used in personal one-to-one communication. Even though email is seen by many as unsexy and maybe even a little old-fashioned, email permissions have many advantages that other types do not.

A mature medium

Email is a mature medium, in the sense that it has been around for many years. Therefore, there are a great many sophisticated systems for sending email, and just as many sophisticated mechanisms to prevent unwanted emails from getting through.

A creative medium – with many rules and exceptions

An email message can be extremely creative in its design. As the sender, you have 100% control over the content. Images, text and even video can be embedded in the mail, so it will be more of an experience than a dry message delivered on a white background. However, with the multitude of devices used for viewing email, there are great differences in how the HTML is rendered. So, as a sender, you must put a lot of work into encoding specific rules and carrying out thorough testing on all devices.

Dynamic content and merge rules

As with direct mail, you have the advantage that you can determine with complete accuracy who, or at least which address, you are sending an email to. Most email service providers offer the opportunity of creating merge rules in your emails, and you can then personalize messages and content according to the information and data you have on your customers. That said, not everyone uses this possibility. The vast majority of email communications that businesses undertake today are of the one-to-many type. This is on an equal footing with traditional print advertising. The difference is simply that it is very inexpensive to deliver.

In addition to varying the content itself, some tools enable the creation of advanced trigger programs, where email messages are sent automatically on the basis of registered events on the part of the customer. The best ones offer this possibility not only for email, but also across several permission types and communication channels. There is more on this in Chapter 4.

Measurability

Email messages have the advantage that virtually any interaction your customers have with them can be tracked. The most common metrics are:

- **bounce rate**: the proportion of sent email messages that could not be delivered
- **open rate**: the proportion of sent email messages that have been opened
- **click rate**: the proportion of sent email messages that have been clicked in
- **conversion rate**: the proportion of sent email messages that resulted in a customer carrying out a desired action (typically a purchase) on the website linked to in the email
- **unsubscription rate**: the proportion of recipients who have opted out of receiving further email from the company
- **spam complaint rate**: the proportion of sent emails marked as spam by the email recipient.

In addition to measuring each type of interaction as a whole, it is becoming more common to record which individuals click on which types of link. This behaviour generates data about the recipient's preferences and interests, which may be used for further communication.

Spam

There are some companies that send marketing-related email messages to recipients who have never given them permission to do so. Either they will send emails to all of their customers with an email address, even if those customers have not given marketing permission, or they will add email addresses to their list via more or less shady methods, such as buying email lists from third parties or automated retrieval via open webpages. This is referred to as 'spam' and it is not a good practice to pursue if you represent a serious business.

Deliverability – will the email get through?

Most browser-based email readers, such as Hotmail and Gmail, have dedicated buttons so that users can report messages as spam. Gmail does not look into whether or not the claim is true. The fact is, however, that if more than a certain percentage of recipients of messages from a particular sender (often measured by IP addresses) declare that they perceive those messages as spam, the sender will be blacklisted. Subsequent email messages from this sender will be suppressed and land in the spam filter. It is therefore a good idea to make it not only possible, which is a legal requirement with GDPR, but also crystal clear how recipients can opt out of unwanted email communication.

It can also be dangerous to wait for too long to use an acquired email permission; perhaps the recipient will not recall having given consent and will mark the message as spam.

Within email deliverability, the term 'bacn' refers to email messages that recipients have given their permission to receive but don't bother to read. It can be argued that, in these cases, if the recipient sees the email in their inbox – even without opening it – the sender has nonetheless attained a brand impression or exposure and thus has created a bit more brand awareness. However, there is usually a more specific message in the email to which the recipient does not respond.

Hotmail and Gmail monitor the amount of bacn a sender generates. If you generally send out a lot of emails that are unopened, then you are gradually punished and your deliverability decreases. They especially punish senders who send to so-called spam traps. Spam traps are email addresses that have been unused for a long time and that Hotmail and Gmail have 'taken back' from the person who originally opened them. If you are sending to spam traps, it is a clear indication that you are not monitoring the quality of your list and do not continuously unsubscribe recipients who don't open communications from you. The problem, of course, is that many marketing employees are rewarded by the number of permissions in the customer database – not the number of active permissions.

To avoid the risk of having your regular internal email end up in spam filters, you should send emails to customers from a different subdomain and IP address than your ordinary domain. For example, if you have the domain Company.com, instead of sending from newsletter@company.com you might send from newsletter@email.company.com.

Browser and desktop notifications

A fairly new permission type is browser notifications. Upon visiting a company's website, the browser or the operating system can be instructed to prompt the user for permission to send them notifications whenever the company deems that something is of interest. YouTube, for instance, uses this type of permission. The format is short and primarily text-based – similar to that of app push notifications. We consider it fairly intrusive and something that brands should use with care. The messages pushed towards end customers should be fairly specific and data driven.

Due to the newness of this communication form, research into the economic potential is fairly limited. Without a doubt, however, it is an extra touchpoint that is bound to cause some kind of awareness. The system support is also relatively limited, and more often than not browser notifications are not a native channel in the common automation marketing solutions out there.

INTIMATE PERMISSION – REALLY UP CLOSE

It vibrates in my pocket – and it's with my consent. It can hardly get more intimate, in terms of contact from a business.

'Intimate permission' is our attempt to conceptualize a contact form that works on an individual level and in quite close proximity – in more than one sense of the term. It is mobile and reaches the customer right where they are by the phone vibrating in their pocket. However, with the potential for such close contact, there is specific best practice for this type of communication.

Text messages

It has been possible to send text messages to customers for many years. Nevertheless, using text messages for marketing is still quite limited compared with email, for several reasons, including:

- Text messages are expensive.
- Text messages are more difficult to track: it is not as easy to track openings and clicks as it is with email.
- Tools for sending text messages often do not provide advanced methods of personalization.
- Opt-out rates for text messages are typically higher than those for email because it is relatively intrusive and also easy to unsubscribe from.
- There is a longer path to an online purchase from a text message than from an email click, even though mobile commerce is growing.

However, text messages do have a very high opening rate.[22] Also, from a purely practical perspective, it is extremely easy to collect phone numbers. There is typically not the same risk of spelling errors as there is in entering and collecting email addresses.

Use with caution

Senders must consider the context in which the user will receive the message. Reception of a text message is most likely followed by either a sound or a vibration. Therefore, senders should consider the timing. A text message in the middle of the night can be highly annoying. You should be especially cautious if you are operating across time zones.

Text messages are typically used as a kind of notification tool with respect to customer inquiries. When will my package be shipped? When is my hairdresser appointment? When should my bike go in for servicing? This has helped to shape consumers' expectations for the channel. To a greater degree than for email, it is expected that the content will be personal and unrelated to sales.

Push messages to an app

Another method of getting closer to customers is by using push notifications to apps that the user already has installed on a mobile device (phone or tablet). It is by its very nature more complicated for customers to download an app, identify themselves by login and then give the app permission to send push messages. It requires a certain closeness of relationship or a really good offer to get this to happen. Your app should contain more customer-oriented and value-adding features than just the capability of receiving messages.

The same precautions about sending times and promotional vrsus service-oriented content that apply to text messaging also exist for app push notifications.

Different degrees of proximity for customer recognition and permission gathering

The closer you get to a customer's intimate sphere, the greater the necessity to think really hard about both the content and the timing of your communication. On a website you can get away with not being particularly relevant without it leading to customer complaints. On a mobile device there is less tolerance of and patience with irrelevant communication. A few irrelevant text messages and the permission and/or customer relationship will be lost.

Lead generation and permissions

Collecting permissions is not necessarily a particularly high-brow, academic discipline. It is in principle a simple proposition to be sold to customers. The key is to give them the offer and make them feel that they will get more out of saying "yes, please" than "no, thanks".

What exactly did I say yes to?

The value proposition does not need to be particularly advanced; in fact, simple messages often work best.

Nordstrom's loyalty programme is called The Nordy Club, and more than 50% of Nordstrom's revenue is accounted for within the loyalty programme.[23] The value proposition for the loyalty programme is as simple as:

Free to join!
Earn points no matter how you pay.
Earn status based on spend.
Reach a new status and enjoy even more benefits, such as priority access to style events.
Get exclusive access.
Enjoy perks such as access to beauty and style workshops, curbside pick-up, first to shop select brands and more.
Earn 1 point per 1 dollar.
Earn points towards Nordstrom Notes, and unlock them even faster with our Nordstrom app.[24]

Note that Nordstrom does not promise any specific discount, aside from earning points that can be used later. Too many companies overestimate the need to give a big discount to get memberships and permissions.

Nordstrom naturally also asks whether it can send communications to customers and its app also prompts users about permission to send push notifications.

We have seen some examples of how, at the time of enrolment, businesses have divided their permissions into many sub-permissions and presented them to the customer up front. This can be a bad idea, because customers typically will never sign up for everything. In unsubscribe scenarios, however, it might be a good idea to provide customers with the option to unsubscribe from specific parts of the communication without having to say no to the whole thing.

PERMISSION GATHERING CAMPAIGNS

Value propositions can be delivered through the channels you already use for communicating with customers.

Permission campaigns via owned media

You don't have to pay to be published on your own media. Therefore, it is natural to use these to a great extent.

The store network

If you have a large store network today, you should activate it from the start. Make it a natural part of sales associates' work to ask customers for their email addresses and possible club membership. Follow up on how well they do it and reward the best. It is the execution that will determine how effective this will be. If it does not become an accepted part of the sales staff's routine, and if the performance is not measured, it can be extremely hard to make it work.

Typically, sales associates have a lot of things they have to remember to ask about in order to support up-sales – for example, "Would you like a box of candy for only €1.50?". In order to use retail as part of collecting permissions, you must have organizational acceptance that a permission is worth far more in the long term than the sale of a box of candy here and now.

Through a store network, you will typically collect permissions among existing customers, so you should primarily collect permissions via this channel with the aim of developing relationships with them. In the context of cultivating brand new customer relationships, this channel's results are limited.

Your website

On your website, you can collect marketing permissions from both potential and existing customers. If you have many unique visitors to your website, it is obvious that you should ask for permission here, but not just in connection with order placement or as a passive call to action. More and more companies are serving up the message about giving permission in a kind of pop-up or overlay triggered by a particular behaviour – for example, time spent on the website or the number of pages shown to the user.

Depending on your business, there can be different opinions for how aggressively you can allow yourself to push the message. Typically, however, it is quite easy to set up the message, as it is often the marketing department that has control over the website.

Email

Talking about the use of email for permission gathering may sound contradictory to many people.

Nonetheless, if you want to extend your reach to customers on as many channels as possible and obtain permission to contact them via either text messages or apps, the email channel is an excellent medium.

Facebook

It is of course possible to use Facebook, particularly in conjunction with campaigns, to collect email permissions. Facebook ads have a special feature for exactly this – but remember that it's paid media and nothing is free.

The fashion retailer Zalando.com is quick to encourage potential customers to make themselves known to the brand on

Facebook (by following the company's page). In return, customers receive offers and even a rebate into the bargain.

Mobile

App and text messages can be used to notify customers if it is found that messages can no longer be sent to the provided email address (i.e. the messages bounce). Text messages in particular can also offer an excellent supplementary way to collect permissions.

In March 2014, the Nordic chain of gas stations Statoil (now Circle K) launched its loyalty concept Statoil Extra. The sometimes overly busy sales associates could not always manage to collect all relevant profile information from the gas station customers, but they could generally manage to get a phone number and enter it into the system. Afterwards, customers would receive up to four text messages reminding them to register for Statoil Extra using the phone registration form. Phones thus worked in combination with the other channels to get members to say "yes, please".

The customer service centre – can't we just ask them when they call?

When customers call your customer centre, it seems like an obvious chance to ask them about marketing permissions for email and mobile. But, before you do so, remember to check with local legislation. Unfortunately, in some territories this is a violation of current law. However, it may still be legal to ask for customers' email address for purposes other than marketing – in fact, with GDPR, you have an obligation to make sure that the information you store about your customers is up to date.

Direct mail – permission gathering via post

A database of customers' physical addresses is still an owned medium, even if it is not as cost-effective to use as for instance emails and push notifications. It is a commonly used tactic to include a message about permission capture as 'envelope stuffing' if you already have the legal obligation to send out postal mailings to customers but do not have marketing permissions.

Permission gathering via paid media

TV campaigns

Paid media is frequently used to collect permissions. A TV ad campaign can easily have a company's loyalty programme as its protagonist and becoming a member as its primary call to action. TV campaigns are expensive, but permission gathering can be incorporated within existing branding-oriented campaigns.

A TV commercial will result in interest in your loyalty programme coming from two directions. Even if your sales staff don't remember to ask customers about membership, there is a chance that the customers will know about the loyalty programme from the TV commercial and will ask about it.

AdWords and banner advertising

An above-the-line mass-media campaign will typically create increased traffic on Google AdWords and other similar services. If there are TV ads running for a loyalty programme, there will also be people looking for the club on search engines. It can be an advantage to advertise on the relevant search words, for example to help the people who are sitting in front of the TV with an iPad on their lap. Likewise, it can make good sense to increase media pressure across channels through banner advertising on various ad networks, including Google and Facebook.

Collecting permissions by leveraging the brand of a supplier

A good way of collecting permissions can be teaming up with a supplier that has an interest in knowing more about how its end customers behave throughout the whole process of shopping. An example of such a collaboration is that between the Dutch online retailer bol.com and LEGO®.

The toy brand LEGO distinguishes between customers and users. Customers are the ones who buy the products (often grown-ups) and users are the ones who actually play with the LEGO bricks (children of all ages). Since LEGO has a policy of not communicating directly with users, it doesn't collect permissions or create personal profiles for users. Instead, it collaborates with its partners (resellers), which engage with the users and collect permissions and data about them.

Together, LEGO and bol.com have set up a dedicated LEGO platform to inspire and better understand users. The result is the video platform speel.bol.com, which offers various types of engaging and interactive content, such as LEGO movies, unboxing videos and user-generated video content – all targeted at children of various ages.

The main goal of the platform is to gather relevant data derived from various touchpoints. This data includes:
1. login data, to provide the companies with demographics and to enable children to post their own created video content and be able to win LEGO products
2. engagement data by adding gamification, such as enabling users to collect LEGO stickers to show they're a big fan of the brand
3. more generic platform statistics, such as traffic numbers and sources, number of video views, time on site and so on.

This data should lead to more relevant insights for both LEGO and bol.com. These insights are used to improve marketing effectiveness and product development (for LEGO) and enhance shop and conversion optimization (for bol.com).

According to Justin Sandee, head of retail media management at bol.com, the numbers are promising. In a personal interview with the authors he revealed that within a relatively short period of time, the platform gathered more than 10,000 unique profiles of children aged 1–11 years. It also appears that children find the platform engaging, with 150,000 video views and 30% of all visitors returning regularly and staying on the platform for 21 minutes on average. Over 2,000 children spent two hours watching videos and earning virtual LEGO badges. These children are rewarded as true LEGO fans, and can share this status with their friends on social media. So far the unboxing videos have been the most popular, especially in the older age groups.

The platform is providing interesting insight into how to adjust the way LEGO products are promoted. The LEGO inspiration platform is a typical example of part of an omnichannel customer approach in which the consumer is put in the middle and their behaviour is the basis for marketing improvements, making LEGO and bol.com more relevant as a brand and a shopping destination.

Collecting permissions from new customers through direct mail and unaddressed mail

Just as traditional direct mail can be a good medium for acquiring digital permissions from existing customers, direct mail or unaddressed mail can also be a means of acquiring permissions from completely new customers. Today, it can be a very liberating feeling to find a letter in the mailbox that is not a bill. As mentioned earlier, the DMA boasts that direct mail has an extremely high opening rate, perhaps precisely because people no longer receive physical mail very often.

But to whom should we send a letter or an unaddressed mailing, when we have all the inhabitants in the world to choose from and the mailing cost is so high? Luckily this information can be bought through providers such as Experian and local vendors. Both business and consumer addresses can be purchased based on a variety of criteria, so you don't have to send expensive direct mail to everybody.

Why doesn't my media agency suggest we do permission campaigns?

Don't forget that most media agencies earn money for media purchases, so they won't push their clients to encourage end customers to convert to their own media instead of paid media. The same applies to advertising agencies. Why would they actively help to saw off the branch they're sitting on? Unless you insist that permission gathering be a completely natural call to action in your mass communication, it will not happen.

MATURITY IN CUSTOMER RECOGNITION & PERMISSIONS

How does a mature business work with customer recognition and permission gathering? Is it unconditionally good to have very many text message permissions and 'less good' to have a great many email permissions? Since there are significant differences in recipients' expectations for communication via websites, email, SMS and app push, healthy communication and service efforts include the effective orchestration of messages *across* channels.

You should use each channel on its own terms and for the types of message most suitable for that medium. It is general practice to send a newsletter via email. If the same communication is suddenly published via text message, then one can expect a significantly inferior performance. However, quite short, personal messages function really well as text messages due to the high opening rate and the physical activation of the device. These can also be sent by email – but not as effectively.

Customer recognition and permission gathering must be practised in line with your existing communication efforts. If you (for reasons to do with prioritizing) have not considered using SMS-based communication, then there is no need to invest massively in collecting permissions to do so. Why send invitations to a party that you're not throwing? But one thing is absolutely certain: working with customer recognition and permission gathering is a key part of omnichannel. Below we have summarized the maturity levels, as we see them in this discipline.

Highest maturity level

The companies that are the most mature in customer recognition and permission gathering work systematically to maintain a large and engaged customer and permission base. They collect several types of permission, including for email, text messages and push messages. Permissions are collected from and integrated across all channels, so there are as many open communication channels as possible for each customer. Customers are automatically recognized across physical and digital channels.

Middle maturity level

Companies with average maturity in working with customer recognition and permission gathering have a focus on building up the volume of their customer and permission base. Permissions are collected across digital channels in particular but are stored in the channel or silo where they are collected.

For example, if phone numbers are collected, they are not necessarily linked to the customer's name, email address or postal address. There is a particular focus on acquiring email permissions and gaining new members of the customer club. Customers are recognized across websites, email and store points of sale.

Lowest maturity level

The companies that work the least maturely with customer recognition and permission gathering can recognize a customer within each channel. Most often this is a task carried out from the website, from cross-exposure on the company's Facebook page or from collecting email addresses. The website uses cookies for simple recognition purposes, and in some cases there is an opportunity to log in. Physical addresses can be found for the customers who have provided them as part of a transaction.

Remember that you can take our test based on the Omnichannel Hexagon and find your company's omnichannel maturity level at:

OMNICHANNELFORBUSINESS.ORG

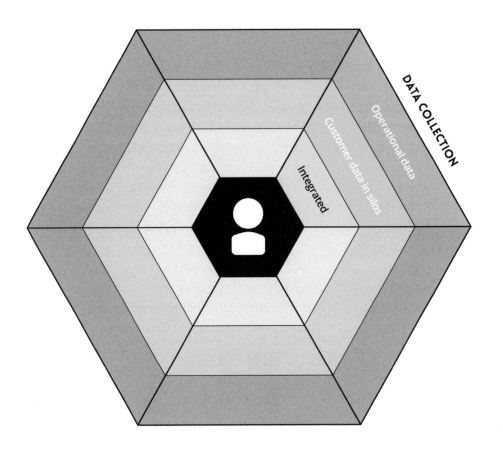

DATA COLLECTION

Operational data

Customer data in silos

Integrated

2

DATA COLLECTION

Data is your company's memory of every single customer and the prerequisite for becoming more relevant in your communication and service. Customer data must be collected systematically and integrated to provide a comprehensive picture of every customer.

Michael's girlfriend was on her period and she was running out of tampons. She asked him to go to the store for her to pick up some more. This seemed like the perfect opportunity for him to visit the new Amazon Go store, a store totally without cashiers – all digital. Except it's a physical store.

At the store he found the doors gated like the entrance to the London Underground. He had to install the Amazon Go app, log in to his Amazon account and scan the app's barcode to enter the store. He almost felt a bit criminal when he picked the tampons from the shelf and put them in his backpack. He looked around and noticed the ceiling was full of cameras that were able to couple the images of him scanning the app and putting specific products into his backpack and add the right products to his bill. He added a few other items to his backpack and left the store.

Suspicious, he took out his phone and opened the Amazon Go app. He was impressed to see that all the items were on the list and that his account had been charged the correct amount. He knew that Amazon was collecting a lot of data on him from his online behaviour and what he'd bought over time, but come to think of it, they must also know a lot about his reading patterns from his Kindle... and his Alexa ... and now this? He couldn't decide whether he was impressed or creeped out – but Amazon definitely made shopping easy.

YOUR COMPANY'S MEMORY OF CUSTOMERS

I f you want your communication to be relevant, then you need to gather data. Data is your business's memory of your customers.

If you take omnichannel seriously, customers must have a seamless experience, even if they change channels along the way while interacting with your business. They must have the sense that information submitted on one channel does not need to be repeated on another and that communication is relevant. Consequently, cross-channel data integration is essential. Interacting with a company that doesn't have data integration is like talking to someone who has had split-brain surgery: the one hemisphere is not connected to the other.

As part of data integration, you must connect your data from each channel to your individual customers – depending on your industry, this may be the case already, to a greater or lesser degree. Speed quickly becomes an important parameter in this integration.

If a customer calls the service centre of their cable company, it will benefit them and the company if the agent has on hand current information, such as that the customer just browsed the website to find information about cancelling their contract and just wrote negatively about the company on Facebook. This will let them know them to speak extra-politely and maybe offer a little extra. In situations like this, timeliness is particularly crucial. This information will not be worth much the next day, when the customer may have cancelled their contract.

There are many different types of data you might collect and integrate. Your customers will be completely aware of submitting some of this data, while other data is more discreetly collected through interaction, particularly on digital channels. This affects how openly you can later use this data in your communication. You don't want your customers to feel monitored – rather, their experience should be one of being helpfully guided by an attentive host who discreetly catches signals and hints.

In this chapter we will address the following:
- what customer data is
- why you should collect customer data
- how data can be classified
- the easiest ways to collect data
- how to store and integrate data
- legal aspects you should consider about data collection.

And finally, we'll present a summary of how the different maturity levels of data collection are classified.

WHAT IS CUSTOMER DATA?

In the field of omnichannel marketing, data is mainly interesting when it can be linked to specific customers. Anonymous customer satisfaction surveys and questionnaire data are therefore irrelevant in this context. They may be used to develop and adjust overall services and communication and to support the development of a general initiative or product, but, in relation to tailoring an individual message to an individual customer at the right time, they are worthless.

Customer data can come from a variety of data sources – mobile devices, customer profiles, questionnaires, previous

purchases, GPS, etc. Some of these are less obvious to customers – for example, clicks and page views on websites and
newsletters are collected, as is data on other digital behaviour.

The amount of data for each customer is growing dramatically
as it becomes more and more common for electronic devices
to measure all kinds of things, from Under Armour tracking
your jogging route to Google's Nest thermostat gauging the
temperature in your home. There are also more unique forms,
specialized for particular users or activities; for example, the
Babolat Play tennis racket can measure how hard you serve or
what percentage of your strokes have topspin.

Imagine if you were able to look up each individual customer
and see all the information your company had available on
them. In today's data-rich world, this would not be a simple
index card that contained basic data. It would contain all the
raw data from every single interaction, transaction, conversation or survey that your company had ever conducted with
this customer. This is something significantly different from
the classic customer record in your customer relationship
management (CRM) system.

Over time, the volume of data collected on each individual
may well reach a considerable size, and by its nature and diver-
sity it can be highly complex. In principle, all collected data
should be saved to ensure the possibility of future analysis.
This has the immediate effect of quickly making the individual
customer's 'profile card' confusing and hard to understand.
Bear in mind though that there is a potential conflict here
between the ambition of collecting and storing almost all data
and the legal requirements in GDPR. According to the GDPR
legislation you are not allowed to store data, unless you can
document how that data is intended to be used and you have
the customer's consent for doing so.

Structured versus unstructured data

Data is sometimes categorized as being 'structured' or 'unstructured'. Structured data is well organized and typically stored in databases and spreadsheets. Records (e.g. of purchase transactions) contain a fixed and known number of fields, and the content of each field will usually be of the same type (e.g. a payment amount or a date). Unstructured data is everything that doesn't fit this simple repeated structure: for example, free text, recordings of speech or other sounds, images, video clips and so on. Some estimates put the proportion of data that is unstructured at 80% or higher, but by its nature it is harder to analyse than structured data. The images Amazon Go's cameras capture of customers in its stores are an example of unstructured data in use, and as you can imagine there is a lot of processing going on behind the scenes to understand and interpret what the cameras are seeing.

Deterministic versus probabilistic data

Another distinction that is important is that between 'deterministic' and 'probabilistic' data. When a specific piece of data – e.g. a transaction – relates to a specific customer in a database, this is called 'deterministic data'. But some data cannot be attributed to an individual with so much certainty. For instance, website visits from a laptop are collected through the use of cookies. But it could be someone else using that laptop (e.g. a child or spouse) so you cannot be completely sure who this data relates to – but you *probably* can, hence the term 'probabilistic'. Later in this chapter, when we look into enriching data through third-party data sources or even into trying to predict customers' characteristics or future behaviour, then we are talking about probabilistic data.

WHY GATHER DATA?

Forgetting for a moment the talk about AI and the fantastic insights one can draw from the huge sum of data assembled from all data sources, what is the data worth in an individual customer relationship?

For it to create any value at all, data needs to be used. A lot of the data that is collected does not require major processing before it can create value with its usage. Take one of the examples introduced above: if you visited your cable company's website for information on how to cancel your contract, it would not take a genius to figure out that you're not the most satisfied customer in the database. The opposite is also true: if you have browsed all possible models of Beolit speakers on Amazon's website, would it be worthwhile for the company to follow up with you? Of course it would.

Owned media is perfect for data collection

Because data is typically collected on owned media, it's often cheaper to collect data than to collect more permissions. Therefore, data collection should be included as a fundamental part of all communication and interaction with customers. See the section on maturity at the end of this chapter for more information.

Permissions are quantity, data is quality

A large permission base has value in that you can reach out to the database on your own initiative and without advertising. Extra customer data carries value in a comparable way as it enables you to personalize the message even further and thus get a better response rate from your customers and ultimately make more money. However, leveraging data to personalize your communication is not without costs; dynamic content and flows for automated communication must be produced and implemented. Data collection is more profitable when the permission base has reached a certain size.

Data as a packaged customer service – quantified self

Data does not just have value as a parameter for segmentation and personalization in communication. Companies have built entire services around customer data. Data is collected, aggregated and displayed to customers because the customers are interested in the data.

This is an example of the megatrend called 'quantified self', which describes a movement where consumers are increasingly interested in monitoring and quantifying everyday behaviour in order to have better control over aspects of their lives such as their workout routines, physical shape and weight. To do this, they monitor their sleep, physical activity and calorie intake. Companies working in this area do business by selling sensors (called 'wearable computing') and/or software and then provide data back to the customer with graphs, statistics, benchmarks for social contacts and so on. Such companies include Garmin, Suunto, Fitbit and Under Armour.

HOW CLOSE TO THE CUSTOMER IS CUSTOMER DATA?

Customer data, just like permissions, can be characterized as being close to or far from the customer. This data can be divided into the following three categories:

1. data on something that the customer has submitted
2. data on something that the customer has done – behavioural data
3. data on what the customer thinks or feels – emotional data.
4. The three degrees of data proximity are summed up in the figure below.

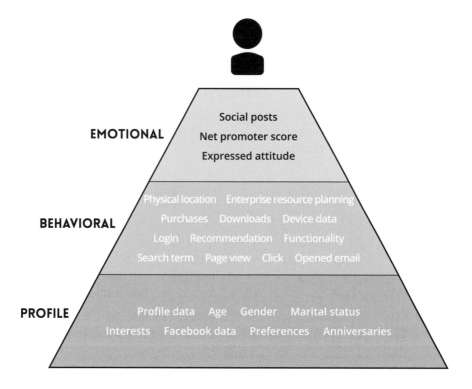

What do customers tell us? Submitted data

Submitted data is that which customers themselves have provided or entered on website forms, in questionnaires, over the telephone or through other means. When granting a permission, signing up for a customer club or entering a customer relationship with a simple customer profile, it is increasingly normal for customers to provide collectable data – name, address, preferences, interests, gender, etc.

The world champion in getting users to enter data about themselves must be LinkedIn. Later in this book, we will look closely at what LinkedIn is doing to get customers to give away this much about themselves.

However, what people say they do in submitted data has the disadvantage of often being different from what they actually do. For example, there can be quite a difference between how often people say that they send someone flowers and how often they actually do it. There can also be differences between how healthily they say they eat and how often they really fall into unhealthy eating habits when they are hungry in the store with a red-hot credit card and an impatient child.

In addition, the submitted data often contains errors or is not very uniform. Whether it is your employees who enter it directly into the CRM or the customers themselves, there are numerous ways of writing 'marketing manager' as a job title (to take one example). In such cases, this information becomes difficult to use for anything on an aggregated level. Thus, you need to develop various tools to normalize and clean the data. See the section "Predicting what we haven't been told" in Chapter 3 for further information on this topic.

What have customers done? Behavioural data

Real behaviour usually says more about our intentions than we ourselves realize. This also applies when you are trying to predict what will be the next step in a customer's lifecycle. Therefore, it is interesting to look at which customer behaviours you can track.

Transactions, emails and clicks

There are numerous sources for collecting information on behaviours, and often they measure purchases or transactions. Behavioural data can also be collected via the email channel. Most email service providers make data available about which recipients have opened or clicked on an email. Among bricks-and-mortar retailers, the impression has typically been that they have to give something back in order for customers to be willing to identify themselves and thus enable the store to link transactions to specific customers. It is in this context that the customer club as we know it today emerged. As we see from Amazon Go and many other grocery stores, convenience can be the compelling reason for customers identifying themselves in a physical store.

Campaign data

Data about which AdWords or banner campaigns a given user has responded to and clicked on is typically sent along as a parameter to the destination website. Within traditional conversion optimization, it is commonly known that the subsequent communication to the user should correspond to the initial message that made the user click the ad. In purely practical terms, this means the campaign message and/or discount is often repeated, so customers will not be in doubt about whether the offer still applies. However, this information is almost always forgotten as soon as the customer closes the browser. However, data on customers' campaign clicks is valuable and you should collect it for later use.

Behavioural data from the website

In recent years, e-commerce businesses have begun sending emails to customers that have left items in their online shopping basket. This is not a bad idea, given that customers often have multiple browser windows open – each containing a webshop – and try to add the same items to each shop's basket in order to gain a real overview of the different prices when shipping, taxes and charges are added in. If nothing comes of this, the store can send a reminder and save the shopping basket.

There are many ways to establish this link, even if the customer is not logged in to the site. If they have clicked on an email link, then cookies can be used to identify the customer. And in all likelihood the retailer can count on future behaviour from that device to be by that particular customer.

There is also the data that customers' presence alone blabs about: multiple tracking systems save the IP address they're using and where in the world they are likely located. Several applications have the capacity to link IP addresses to corporate databases and determine what company they come from. This is extremely useful in B2B sales, for instance.

Behaviour can give us an idea of the direction in which a (potential) customer is headed.

All too often, however, the data is *not* collected on the website. Keep in mind that Google Analytics does not make individuals' data available; it only displays data at an aggregated statistical level. This may in itself be extremely useful to analyse, but in one-to-one dialogue with a customer it cannot be used to trigger or personalize content. With other tools and techniques (including page tagging, packet sniffing and log analysis), it is possible to capture detailed 'clickstream' data at the level of the individual visitor. This data is complex and potentially vast, but there are techniques that can extract useful and actionable insights from it. (See Chapter 3 for a description of sequence detection.)

Data from customer service centres and chat

Larger companies typically have a customer service centre that allows customers to call in. Data on such calls can be recorded in some form of CRM system, perhaps including specific information on what the conversation was about and the outcome. If your company has a phone menu, calls may be automatically classified in relation to this structure. Calls may in many cases be linked up to the calling telephone number (by caller ID) and thus to the customer's profile, otherwise the service employee should ask for and properly record the data.

The whole point of customers calling in is that they can get service and, hopefully, answers to their questions right away. In a slightly longer-term perspective, however, it is interesting to gather this data and incorporate it into your company's data models. Which customers have called? In connection to what? How often does each customer call? Were they more or less satisfied after the call? In some cases, calls are recorded as audio files and thus become part of an organization's unstructured data.

Chat is interesting in the same context – for example, like call data, it is not as structured as purchase data. It is in text format, so on the aggregate level and with the right techniques it can be used to find connections and correlations.

The Internet of Things – data from devices

As mentioned earlier, the explosion in the number of online devices means that there are more potential data sources all the time. Take, for instance, Tesla. Every car it makes is in effect a computer on wheels. Each car is collecting detailed information about the customer's speed, position, direction, surroundings, etc. This data is necessary for the self-driving capabilities that these cars offer, but it also says a lot about the drivers. Where do you live? Work? Shop?

What do customers feel? Emotional data

Data on behaviour and expressed interests may be misleading. What we really want to know is how customers think or feel. If only we could measure it! You're not going to get permission to shoot a chip into the neck of even your most loyal customers. So what options do you have?

Questionnaires

You can ask your customers what they think. This is seen more and more often, particularly among telecom companies. As will be elaborated upon in Chapter 5, every call centre interaction with Telenor (a Norwegian multinational telecommunications company) results in customers being asked to what extent they are willing to recommend Telenor to a friend or colleague. The company has the option of getting back to customers to instruct them how to go about making a recommendation, if such willingness is expressed, or to try and remedy whatever caused a negative opinion, if that was the case.

Sentiment analysis

Sentiment analysis is the practice of determining whether the issuer of an oral or written statement is feeling positive, negative or even disappointed or excited about the topic. In practice, this measurement can be carried out on received emails or Facebook messages, public posts on Twitter and Facebook, and survey responses.

Keep in mind, though, that sentiment analysis can have a hard time spotting sarcasm and may end up interpreting heavy sarcasm at face value. It also can't be reliably addressed using simplistic matching of keywords or terms. For example, for telecom companies, a customer mentioning dropped calls might be expected to be complaining, but if they made a statement such as "since I switched to you from Telecom X, I've had fewer dropped calls," that would convey a positive sentiment. Sentiment analysis should involve heavy data analytics – see Chapter 3 for more on this.

Data collection in the future

In the future, it will not be enough to rely on how people respond to a questionnaire or what they write on social media. Translated into an everyday metaphor, we can say that we are interested in customers' digital body language: the better we are at decoding it, the greater our understanding of them.

Apart from analysing the text, already there are effective ways of understanding the emotions that lie behind what a customer says. For years, insurance companies have been using voice stress analysis on customer conversations to help spot potentially fraudulent claims. The same technology can tag the recorded text of a conversation on any topic and may be able to detect that someone very patiently and politely telling a call centre agent about how their product keeps failing is actually seething with rage and therefore at risk of leaving the business as a customer.

In the future there will certainly be better capabilities of measuring what customers are thinking. It will be interesting to see how far we get with the gradual adoption of wearable computing. If people are all surrounded by the 'Internet of Things' while wearing sensors, then in principle we will be able to measure what they are looking at and its effect on their pulse. Then we will have a very strong indication of what interests them and what they ignore. The prospects are at once inspiring and frightening.

ENRICHMENT WITH THIRD-PARTY DATA

In addition to being interested in the data that you have on your customers, you should consider that there is great value to be found in third-party data. For example, business databases such as Dun & Bradstreet propose to enrich your database with business information such as revenue, turnover and number of employees. The same is true for households, where Experian and similar companies can give you statistical information about each address. There is no guarantee it will be accurate as such, but it will give you an idea of each customer's likely attributes. It is probabilistic data and should be good enough to give you at least at hint of how your customer database is put together and which segments you could consider in your marketing. In the absence of firm information at the individual level, it can enable you (with caution!) to make a 'best guess'.

In-market data – from other parties' websites

But what if you have very little traffic on your own website and you want to leverage data from how people are generally browsing the internet? What if you knew that some of your football-crazed customers were starting to browse websites indicating that a baby would soon be entering the world? Couldn't you somehow collect this data and send them emails with baby stuff? In theory it is possible to integrate probabilistic segments based on behaviour on third-party websites through a data management platform into your owned media ecosystem. We haven't been fortunate enough to come across any hard evidence that companies are already doing this, but expect to see this in the future sometime soon.

COLLECTING CUSTOMER DATA

We have taken a thorough look at the types of data that can be collected, whether this is something that a customer has submitted, done, or thinks or feels. In practice, how can you collect all this data? And how do you best use it once it has been collected? In the omnichannel world, data should preferably be available in real time across all other channels.

A track record for collecting massive amounts of data

The best indicator of how much customer data a company collects is the amount of data that is necessary for fundamental business processes such as billing and accounting. This means that there are big differences in how companies have been collecting data historically. Telecom and banking companies have abnormally large and detailed amounts of data: on calls, texts, data traffic, etc. for the former, and on each and every account, every single transaction and movement in the currency exchange, and in currencies and stocks for the latter. Next come companies that offer their services via subscription. These companies have a natural reason to gather data and thus have a head start when doing data analytics, particularly when their services by their nature involve a high level of customer engagement.

The downside of having collected data for years

Often, once data has been collected, it lies in various silos around the organization, often on older platforms where data access and integration with other systems may be technically challenging. In such organizations it is still possible to find systems that are 'closed' on the weekends and whose original developers have retired. This can make it really hard to set up any kind of omnichannel activity on this basis. When the decision is made to go omnichannel, it often requires a significant investment for companies with a lot of legacy data and systems.

COLLECTING DATA THAT CUSTOMERS HAVE SUBMITTED

LinkedIn, a professional social network with over 500 million profiles,[25] is undisputedly one of the best companies at getting users to submit personal data. Profiles are often detailed, with everything from skills to former and current workplaces to CVs. In addition, users can create posts (like on Facebook) and blogs (like on Tumblr).

LinkedIn has succeeded in getting all users to manually enter data about themselves. There are three main reasons for this.

1. Create motivation to submit data

To write and maintain a CV that is nicely formatted, containing recommendations and other features, is a cumbersome manual process. LinkedIn provides the advantages of having all this information in one place, where it is always available for potential headhunters. This point is stressed by LinkedIn, which makes users aware of how many people (and who) have viewed their profile within a recent period. LinkedIn appeals to users' exhibitionism or self-consciousness as an incentive to update their CVs.

2. Make it easy to submit data

Even if the incentive to enter information is there, any sense of the data submission process being slightly inconvenient can act as a barrier to doing so. Therefore, LinkedIn has lavished attention on its interface and fine-tuned the user-friendliness of its forms.

Not all data needs to be collected at one time; it can be accumulated continually. The idea is that in every newsletter there is a simple question that the recipient can respond to by simply clicking. It works best if the question is related to one of the topics in the newsletter.

3. Use gaming techniques to motivate submission of more data

You've probably even seen a percentage showing how complete your LinkedIn profile is. 'Profile completeness' is a trick borrowed from gamification, based on the human tendency to want to complete things. By displaying that your profile is only 80% complete, then specifying what it will take to reach the next 5%, LinkedIn appeals to your basic instinct to complete something you started.

Main points with respect to collecting submitted data

The list below includes the key points for consideration with respect to collecting the data submitted by customers. LinkedIn uses them all – with the exception of the last, 'use of incentives'. That's a very popular one, though – most loyalty programmes work with customers earning points for extra engagement.

- Make it very easy to fill in data.
- Write good help pages for users to access.
- Do not ask for all the data at once, but work with continual profiling.
- Ask for permission to connect with customers' social media profiles.
- Use gaming tactics that tease users to submit more.
- Show profiles to customers on an ongoing basis so they become aware of any changes.
- Consider using incentives in the form of points, gifts and participation in competitions.

COLLECTING BEHAVIOURAL DATA

Although Amazon still has limited reach in the physical space and limited amounts of data from this channel, Amazon Go has set the bar for how data can be collected in-store.

So let's jump into it. What is Amazon doing to collect behavioural data about its customers? And what are the frontrunners among the traditional retail outlets doing?

Collecting website data without login

In situations where you have email permission from the user but no login, an option is to set a cookie on the user the first time they visit your site through an email message that you send to them. In this way you can collect behavioural data from this lead with fairly high accuracy. However, keep in mind that this is still probabilistic data.

Motivate login

When you are logged in, Amazon can be more certain of your identity. Therefore, the login box calls attention to itself when you first open the page. The box's second suggestion is that you create a profile.

Aside from allowing Amazon to be more certain that it is you browsing its pages, a login on a new device provides the company with an opportunity to get a comprehensive picture of your behaviour across devices. So, if you've suddenly logged in on a phone, they can stitch together the two behavioural tracks.

Similar tactics are used in B2B lead generation. By tempting customers with a free download of a white paper, customers are encouraged to submit their identifying details, and then the entire behavioural history for the device is linked to the right individual.

Persistent login

Amazon remembers that you are logged in, and, since it also has your payment information, the company can make it very easy for you to complete a purchase. Even if you're not quite ready to make a purchase today, Amazon ensures that it collects and saves data from your visit for next time.

It is very simple: stop asking your customers to log in every single time. If you have sensitive functions that need to be further protected, then you may be able to take advantage of multiple security zones. For example, ask for the password again if the customer tries to make a purchase. But don't throw all the juicy click-data away because your IT department preaches greater security.

Create a service that users love but where you get the data

You may not know it, but Amazon owns the IMDB.com (Internet Movie Database) film community. IMDB contains rich information on films produced worldwide. It is a focal point for any movie lover and is used to answer all the typical questions, such as: "What was that other film I saw that actor in?" or "How good do other people think this movie is?".

Every time a user visits IMDB.com, data is shared with Amazon. Thus, you should not be surprised if you get offers from Amazon based on your browser history with IMDB. And IMDB is just one example of how a brand has made (or bought) a service that is in itself value-creating for customers and will be used to gain knowledge about them.

A more overt example is Nike's service Nike+, which started as a running community. Today Nike+ lives in an app and offers training programmes and virtual trainers. Through the use of the service, customers interact more with Nike, and the brand becomes more strongly linked with training in their minds. In addition, Nike uses data for both product development and marketing – see for yourself at Nike's Privacy Policy.[26]

Behavioural data from stores

At the time of writing this book, the number of Amazon Go's stores is still limited. Even as this type of shop becomes more popular and you consider implementing similar tools to those used in Amazon Go stores, you may find that you do not have the same budget for in-store cameras and AI. So let's have a look at other ways of collecting data in-store.

Loyalty programmes for capturing data

Loyalty programmes are the most common way to get customers to register purchases. One of the best-known examples is that of the British supermarket giant Tesco, which launched its loyalty card in 1995. Tesco has data from over 13 million British consumers who have faithfully used its Clubcard for years. The card offers customers a 1% discount on their purchases in the form of points, which are paid out quarterly in the form of vouchers that can be used to buy more in Tesco's stores or from its many partners.

The primary value for Tesco is not that customers visit its stores more often for the 1% discount. The real value is that Tesco collects data from customers every time they make a purchase. When analysed, this data provides valuable information and can be used for business development.

Collect data using the customer's phone

Waitrose takes in-store data collection one step further. Like many other retailers that have gradually come to realize that we will soon not have room for more loyalty cards in our wallets, Waitrose offers an app instead of a physical card.

Customers scan their items one by one as they are placed in the basket (and even directly into bags). Customers can then check out and pay without the goods being handled by an employee and without going through checkout process, with all its manual work of standing in line and moving, scanning and packing the goods.

It is also possible to collect data on store proximity or even precise positioning within a department store by combining app and beacon technology. If you missed it, then head back to Chapter 1 for more on this topic.

Mobile point-of-sale systems

You should include store staff in your strategy for data collection. The interaction between staff and customers at the point of sale is a great opportunity to collect data – especially if the product is of such a nature that it requires further consideration before a final purchase. In this case, the staff together with the customer can make an offer – essentially, put together a shopping basket – and link it to the customer's profile. The customer can then quietly make the final decision at home, perhaps in consultation with their spouse or some friends.

An example of this is IKEA, where staff help customers to configure a dream kitchen on the store's kitchen app. The design is saved on the customer's own profile and can be retrieved later, when the customer is further along in the purchase process. Scandinavian furniture company Bolia applies the same technique in-store. The exact configuration of a sofa is saved in a digital basket and customers are reminded later. Needless to say, the rates at which such activities are turned into purchases are quite impressive.

Increasingly, the trend is moving towards customer self-service, with staff time instead being used to guide and advise customers. For example, in Burberry's stores, sales associates invite customers to identify themselves on iPads, which are then used as a basis for discussion and advice based on previous purchases – both in-store and online product collections. If the customer is ready to make a purchase, the transaction can be carried out right there on the couch in the store, where the customer is sitting comfortably, enjoying being advised and served. Burberry decorates its stores so that the purchase experience is just as comfortable as sitting at home with your laptop – this is a chance to have professional service and advice into the bargain, as well as an opportunity to try on clothes before your card is swiped.[27]

Build data collection into the product

There are countless examples of how data collection can be built into products. Of course, there are digital products – Netflix, Spotify, Storytel and such. These collect data as a totally natural and integrated part of using the service. However, some physical products collect data too. A few examples include the Amazon Kindle reader, the Babolat Play Tennis Racket, Tesla cars and even Vestas windmills. The brands behind these products gain vital insights and knowledge from customers' interaction with their products, for use on both an aggregate level and a personal level. It takes great maturity within organizations to not only build this data into the product but also make the data available for marketing and communication purposes.

It is also worth mentioning Under Armour and its Connected Fitness product line. This is an example of an otherwise traditional apparel brand at the mercy of resellers' decisions about whether to display and position its products. By developing and launching a digital product, Under Armour gained direct access to end customers and the ability to collect data from those customers to help foster real brand love. The large customer/user community has also become a revenue stream in itself, with Under Armour offering partners opportunities to sponsor branded challenges for members.

Behavioural data from other parties

Since most of their brand interactions happen within the ecosystems of their resellers or partners, CPG (consumer packaged goods) companies can find direct customer data collection to be a difficult and slow process. Instead of doubling down on owning the touchpoints, it can be a good strategy to directly team up with resellers and partners to exchange data. This is exactly how Disney collaborates with movie theatres and retailers in the US. Through partnerships, Disney builds customer profiles and collects data on who has seen which movie or purchased which toy. It gives the company a much faster timeframe for collecting enough customer data to make the use of it profitable.

CAPTURING CUSTOMERS' EMOTIONS

Good examples of companies that systematically collect data on what customers think and feel are few and far between. We mentioned earlier how companies can use sentiment analysis to measure what customers who contact their call centres, and use chat and social media, think and feel.

With the exception of Under Armour, Fitbit, Apple Watch and other wearable technology providers, most international examples we have identified have the disadvantage of only measuring the customers who are involved in active dialogue or engagement with the brand. This means that most companies only have access to data through interactions with customers or by asking them directly how they feel.

INTEGRATION AND STORAGE

All the juicy data collected from customers is not worth much if you do not use it. As Chapter 4 explains in detail, data can be used directly with customers in one-to-one communication, creating an experience of closeness and strengthening the relevance of the communication. If the data source and the communication channel are not the same, then integration will naturally be required. Does one channel get to know what is happening in another? How quickly does this happen in practice? Integration and timing suddenly become hugely important.

Data silos

Today, most companies are present on multiple channels and media. For example, a company may have established a chain of stores, a website, an app, a customer club with an email newsletter and a Facebook account; it may also provide service over the phone and by chat. Each of these presences is both a communication channel and a source of data. Most of the time, data collected in a certain channel can be used to personalize messages in that channel. But, if data is not integrated with other channels, then we are talking about data silos.

IT and finance silos

In a classic large company, each channel is typically anchored in its own department. The finance department is responsible for the sales data; otherwise, it cannot settle accounts. Typically, data access and processing are rooted in the IT department, and data is treated as business-critical. There is thus good control and monitoring of backups, access, security, etc. However, it is far from certain that the data has any connection to individual customers, because this has typically not been necessary in order to carry out proper accounting.

IT departments typically have plenty to do to ensure that ERP (enterprise resource planning) systems are running as they should. Quite often the IT department has its very own physical server set up for the ERP system and, in some cases, the IT function is shared among multiple subsidiaries. If the company has been through mergers and acquisitions, or if there are different types of stores (e.g. franchises and proprietary shops), there is often not just one ERP system, but several.

Replacing or merging ERP systems can take several years and often requires blood, sweat and tears. In the meantime, integrating data for use in either e-commerce or marketing is not the highest item on the priority list. The first priority is to make sales and keep accounts; everything else is secondary.

Marketing and all its systems

Marketing has traditionally not had much data. This has, however, changed considerably in the past decade. Until recently, it was quite normal for IT departments to have responsibility for company websites. Today, nine times out of ten it is the marketing department that has this responsibility. It may well be that IT still maintains hosting, but marketing is increasingly involved in building and developing websites. It is also often marketing that is responsible for sending newsletters to customers, creating dialogue with customers on the company's Facebook page and maybe also developing an app.

There is significant pressure from customers and there will be internal expectations about how many and which platforms the company should be present on. And often it is not difficult to create a new presence on a new channel, whether a simple newsletter or the latest social network. Integration is often not questioned until after the basic setup has been completed, and that is often too late. The app was built cheaply and not built to exchange data. The same is the case with the email system and IT has no time to help with the website because it is about to upgrade the ERP system.

Since it's hard to get data integration prioritized, the use of data is often suboptimal. In a fairly normal scenario, emails are only personalized with data that is already in the system. Once in a while, data from the CRM system, customer club or website is imported manually for use in a campaign with little better impact than the usual conversion rate.

Integration is difficult and this harms the customer experience

If the IT, customer service and marketing departments each have their own systems where they store data and have no compelling incentives to help each other, integration between the systems will be nonexistent. The experience for a customer will be that customer service and marketing will not know what products were purchased. Marketing will not know that the customer is unhappy, and the staff at the store will offer 'good deals' when better deals can be found in their own newsletter. IT and finance may have good systems, but they will have to face the fact that there are fewer and fewer sales to record and report on, because they are losing their customers to more omnichannel-focused competitors.

Modern IT departments have a data warehouse

Perhaps due to GDPR legislation, IT departments have become more aware of consolidating all data across the enterprise. It is now common for a company to have a data warehouse – a system that gathers data and exposes it through APIs (application programming interfaces) or business services. A data warehouse is not necessarily built for the sake of marketing or analytics, but it represents a much better state than prior to GDPR.

OMNICHANNEL INTEGRATION AND CUSTOMER PROFILES

In an omnichannel scenario, the IT department helps to integrate data that the marketing and customer service departments can use in their functions. New data sources are connected to one hub for all customer data, known as a 'single customer view' or a 'customer profile'.

The customer profile is a gathering place for data that is important for interaction with the customer in the near future. It is *not* a complete collection of all data ever collected from the customer, but rather of the most important historical interactions, master data and purchase history (i.e. more or less static data). Added to this is newer and more dynamic interaction data: what has the customer read on the website or in the newsletter recently? What has the customer been talking about with customer service? What is in their online shopping basket right now? If the interaction was over a month ago, it has probably lost its importance to communication and service in the near future.

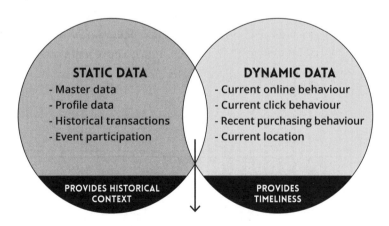

STATIC DATA
- Master data
- Profile data
- Historical transactions
- Event participation

DYNAMIC DATA
- Current online behaviour
- Current click behaviour
- Recent purchasing behaviour
- Current location

PROVIDES HISTORICAL
CONTEXT

PROVIDES
TIMELINESS

CUSTOMER PROFILE
A single place to access customer
data for automated and manual
service and communication

Beyond this simple data, the customer profile can contain more complex, calculated insights, for example the next best action or the risk of churn. Read more about this in Chapter 3.

The full customer profile, with all marketing-relevant data available, normally resides in a dispersed form throughout the 'marketing cloud' that is used by companies. Alternatively, it may be stored in what is now called a 'customer data platform' or similar.

Customer data platforms

The CDP (customer data platform) is a fairly new category of system. CDPs are marketing-controlled data platforms that hold all the data marketers need. They can hold data on both known and unknown customers and make it possible for marketers to build and manage dynamic segments using both business rules and AI, and then to supply communication platforms with these insights. Some also hold the possibility of actually executing communications through campaigns and automated communication flows.

Data management platforms

Although the name 'data management platform' (DMP) may suggest an entity that is similar to the data warehouse or CDP, a DMP is something quite different. A DMP is somewhat similar to a CDP, but it is entirely focused on optimizing the use of paid media.

It can integrate all kinds of data from first-party data sources such as CRMs and e-commerce systems, and combine this with 'in-market' data sources consisting of anonymous cookie audiences enriched in numerous ways.

OMNICHANNEL DATA COLLECTION – WHERE DO I START?

A great place to start is to take inspiration from how LinkedIn gets customers to enter data, and the way Amazon and other forward-looking retailers collect behavioural data both from digital channels and in-store. It will be good practice to build data collection into your product and consider how you might gather emotional data by systematically asking customers for it, via either questionnaires or advanced measurements.

Data from surveys, websites, email, customer clubs, etc. is often quite easy to collect and integrate. At least, this is the case if you use tools that are not monolithic systems but are built for integration – both data in and data out.

LEGAL ISSUES WITH DATA COLLECTION AND STORAGE

All customer data is in principle personal data and EU consumers are protected under GDPR. The California Consumer Privacy Act looks after Californians and Canada has its Anti-Spam Legislation. Similar laws exist in other countries and you should remember to take these into account before you throw yourself into the big data-collection circus.

As a general rule, you should seek consent for direct communication as well as for storing and processing personal data on your customers. It has to be clear which data you are collecting and with which purpose.

Personal data can be divided into two broad categories:
1. general personal data
2. sensitive personal data.

General personal data contains identification and information on names, titles, transactions, the customer relationship and other non-sensitive items. Information is considered to be public when it is public for a wide circle of people. On this basis, you should be able to consider all data submitted to Facebook or LinkedIn, for example, as being 'public' and therefore alright to collect and use.

Sensitive personal data is information about race and ethnicity, political opinions, religious or philosophical beliefs, trade union membership, health records and sexuality, as well as criminal records, information about major social problems and intra-familial relationships.

According to GDPR, customers have the right to know (by request) exactly what data a company has collected on them and also has the right to have this data deleted (or at least anonymized).

At the time of writing, we do not know of any companies that have been convicted of a breach of any of these laws. What scares many companies is the upper limit of the potential fines. These can amount to as much as 4% of global revenue.

MATURITY IN DATA COLLECTION

Although emotional data provides a deep view of a customer's experience, it is not necessarily the most profitable data type for a company to collect, and it is not necessarily wise to give up on submitted and behavioural data. So, what represents maturity in the field of data collection?

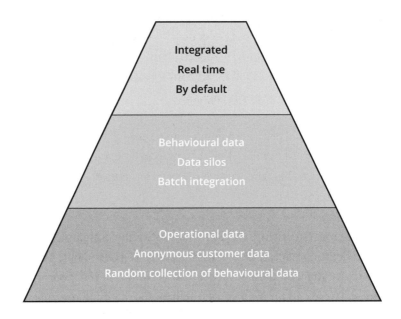

Integrated
Real time
By default

Behavioural data
Data silos
Batch integration

Operational data
Anonymous customer data
Random collection of behavioural data

Highest maturity level

The companies that are the furthest along in their data collection maturity work systematically to collect and centralize submitted, behavioural and emotional data across all customer-facing activities, whether on physical or digital channels. Mature companies have only one profile for each customer, where the main data for them is summarized and can easily be accessed from other systems and by any employee in the company. These companies have 100% control over their own privacy policy and the laws related to personal data.

Middle maturity level

At the middle maturity level are companies that frequently collect both submitted and behavioural data and save it on the individual level. The data collection takes place on several different channels – physical and digital – but is only integrated to a small extent and not at all centralized, either between organizational departments or between channels. Any integration is most often achieved by either manual uploading of files or nightly batch transfers between channels.

Lowest maturity level

On the lowest data collection maturity level are businesses that collect data for the sole purpose of record-keeping for accounting purposes, as prescribed by law. They do not work systematically at gathering different types of data on customers. The marketing data that is collected is not generally linked to or saved on the individual customer level, whether it is from questionnaires, the website or completed in-store purchases. If there is data that can be linked to a specific individual customer, it is random and not indicative of a genuine priority.

Remember that you can take our test based on the Omnichannel Hexagon and find your company's omnichannel maturity level at:

OMNICHANNELFORBUSINESS.ORG

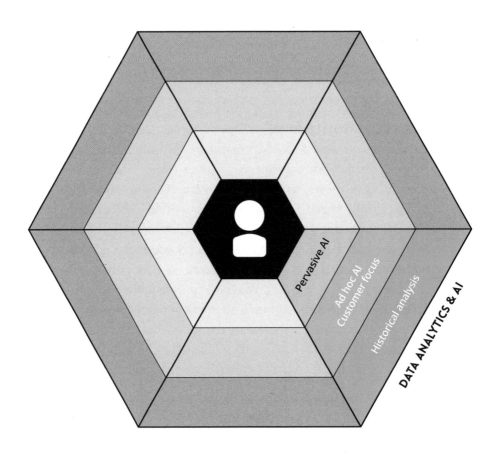

Pervasive AI

Ad hoc AI
Customer focus

Historical analysis

DATA ANALYTICS & AI

3

DATA ANALYTICS & AI

Having direct access to data during customer interactions is valuable and enables a personalized approach. Using analytics and AI on the underlying data, though, can take us even further. Advanced analytical techniques can use any or all available data to *recommend* – or *specify* – what action to take in any interaction.

Martin works for Storytel, an audiobook and ebook company, heading a rapidly growing department working with data analytics. Storytel's customers pay a flat monthly fee and can consume as many books as they like. With a fast-growing customer base of currently more than 700,000, Storytel has access to heaps of data. Every single digital interaction is recorded on a granular customer level.

One of Martin's first projects with the company was to develop and set up a book score that would determine the optimal books for each customer – not only considering the relevance of the book but also the length, the cost and other factors as well. This dramatically reduced the cost base while raising customer loyalty. The books that people chose from these recommendations even had a higher chance of getting read to the end than did books that people searched for themselves. Ever since then, data analytics has been a central part of Storytel's business.

Today Martin is starting on the next planned task of the company's analytics journey. His team already analysed the preliminary clustering of the different ways people use the app. They used algorithms to understand how different data points appeared in clusters. The data enabled them to recognize and label typical usages of the service. There was a clear cluster of data that indicated heavy usage during commuting hours and while a listener was moving. Another showed people using the service for long periods of time in the evening, and another consisted of people using it just before bedtime for titles for children aged between five and ten years.

Martin will instruct his team to set up ongoing scoring of all customers, tagging them with which cluster they resemble the most and enriching each customer record in the automation system with this insight. This will enable the CRM (customer relationship management) team to become even more relevant.

The next big project will use data analytics to identify the 'next best action' for each customer. The data will assemble a range of options for what could be communicated to a customer or done for them. Algorithms will tell the company what is the best thing to do next in order to keep satisfaction high and subscription cancellations low.

S torytel's ability to tailor its communication and service to individual customers stems not just from the raw data it collects and holds but also from applying advanced analytical techniques that give the company the insights it needs to understand each customer in detail and the foresight to accurately anticipate customers' preferences and desires.

Insights and foresights can be extracted and applied from complex data using advanced analytics and AI. This information can drive individually personalized, relevant communication; traditional analytics involving KPIs (key performance indicators; see Chapter 5), dashboards, forecasts and the like simply can't take you to that level. The challenge for chief marketing officers new to this level of analytical technology is twofold: to understand how and where it can most effectively boost marketing effectiveness and how best to bring it into their operations.

In this chapter, we'll aim to demystify the techniques and technologies involved, so you can understand the capabilities they provide to marketers and imagine how they could add value to your marketing. We'll provide guidelines for how you should plan your adoption of AI and advanced analytics to maximize your chances of success and achieve quick value. We'll also take you through (in detail) how you can use the approaches we've described here to transform traditional marketing tasks. We'll finish with a look to the future – which, in this rapidly developing area, is here today for organizations with the imagination and vision to go for it!

Realizing that data analytics and AI is probably the discipline least known to marketers, in this chapter we will use narratives a bit more to further strengthen the understanding with our readers.

AND BIG DATA BEGAT ...

Many of the techniques in AI and advanced analytics have been around for decades, but in most of that time they've only been used by relatively small numbers of visionaries and early adopters.

Around 2010, the term 'Big Data' became prominent. It fired the imaginations of many who had never before seriously considered the opportunities that could be opened up by making their organizations data driven. Although there was no single accepted definition of Big Data – it was loosely defined in terms of the volume, variety, velocity and veracity of the data involved – senior executives realized there was huge potential in their data assets. For the first time, many of them were open to investing in technologies and initiatives to exploit that potential.

While that was undoubtedly a good thing, the problem was that most of these senior executives – and the champions and teams they assigned to create and drive their Big Data projects – had little or no idea of how to achieve this value. In a hype-laden market, vendors pushing the adoption of data management and analysis tools were advising potential adopters: "Just dive into your data lake, and you'll find lots of valuable insights that will transform your business!" This approach ignored what analytics practitioners had known for years – that the vast majority of patterns and correlations in any given data set simply have no business significance.

Misguidedly diving into data led to the disillusionment of many early adopters when their initial projects failed to deliver significant (or any!) value. Others who adopted the approach already used by successful analytics practitioners fared better.

They understood that analysis needs to be directed by specific business goals. The process involves:

- identifying outcomes that can be improved to achieve these goals
- considering the decisions that need to be optimized to give those improved outcomes
- working out what analytical approaches can drive those better decisions
- understanding to what data those analyses should be applied.

This 'business first' approach focuses on steps to deliver (and measure) value and underlies the genuine successes from the Big Data era.

Big Data blended seamlessly into the next wave: AI (artificial intelligence). AI subsumes the data-based and analytical technologies of Big Data while enabling even broader possibilities for adding machine intelligence to business operations. But it's still as easy to embark on initiatives that are data driven and end up as 'science projects' with no proven value and a legacy of disappointment. As always, it's crucial that projects focus on business imperatives – in the case of marketing, driving the best possible outcomes across all stages of the customer lifecycle. When taking the first step in AI, it is crucial to keep this in mind.

ARTIFICIAL INTELLIGENCE

AI is not new. Researchers were working in this area as far back as the 1950s. The high-level definition is simple: if a computer does something that can be done by a human, something we would say was 'intelligent' – then it is exhibiting AI.

AI covers many areas, including robotics, machine vision, natural language processing and synthesis, planning, and problem-solving. The area that is at the heart of most applications of AI today is 'machine learning'. This is an umbrella term for algorithms that can consider historical data, work out what's been going on and apply their findings to make accurate and robust assessments of current and future cases.

Machine learning is tremendously relevant to marketing. With today's consumers generating huge and complex masses of data, it is impossible for human marketers to successfully 'learn' the shifting patterns that indicate preference and likely behaviour. This is the aspect of AI we're considering here.

There's analytics ... and there's *analytics*!

Marketing departments have always worked with data. AI, with its machine learning capabilities, shouldn't be thought of as something that stands apart from the analysis work marketers already do; rather, it's best to think of analysis as a continuum of approaches, techniques and technologies, in which 'conventional' analysis blends seamlessly into advanced analytics and AI.

Descriptive analytics includes traditional statistics, but in business it is more likely to involve calculations on spreadsheets, queries against databases, and generation of business intelligence reports and dashboards. These all provide a 'rear-view-mirror' perspective, looking back at what has been going on up to this point in time. Business intelligence will often aggregate data up to KPIs; it is up to the user to drill down into these KPIs, manually exploring the data to find any relevant underlying patterns.

Visualization tools can also be considered an aspect of descriptive analytics, as they provide the ability to explore and understand current or historical data. Visualizations range from simple, static charts – the pie charts, histograms, etc. available in spreadsheets – to highly interactive and dynamic displays of multi-dimensional data that you can fly through in an experience akin to virtual reality!

Forward-looking analysis is not new, but to date this has mainly involved forecasting. This is a 'headline-level' approach based on past trends and patterns: where are revenues, profits, retention rates, etc. going? Forecasts are great for gaining a general understanding and can be effective tools for overall planning, but they don't bring us anywhere near the level of detail needed for personalization of individual communications and interactions.

Predictive analytics also start from historical data, but in this case machine learning algorithms automatically explore data to find underlying patterns and relationships that relate to specific business outcomes, such as the propensity of a customer to purchase a particular type of product. These patterns are insights that marketers can use, but the algorithms also produce something directly actionable: 'models', which can assess any current or new case and automatically predict its outcome. Predictive models return a simple assessment of each case, often a number that is a propensity or score. These models can also be used as the basis of forecasting – for example, aggregating predicted per-customer risk of churn can be used to show the overall trend to expect. Unlike in the 'headline' approach, though, users can drill into the overall figure – effectively a 'key performance predictor' (KPP) – to see the outcomes predicted for groups or individuals.

Prescriptive analytics turns the output of a predictive model – for example, a 'score' for how likely an outcome is – into a directly actionable decision, by combining that score with business logic to decide the best thing to do in each case (e.g. whether to deliver an offer, what that should be and through which channel it should be delivered).

Because predictive and prescriptive analytics are based around machine learning, they can be considered to fall under the umbrella of AI. In this book, we'll often simply use 'AI' to describe these advanced levels of analytics.

Advanced analytics (indeed, the whole continuum of techniques) can be applied to any area of the business (risk, finance, network planning, operations, supply chain, etc.) where there is data that, through analysis, can inject intelligence into decisions to drive better outcomes. Even the range of application areas related to marketing is extensive: sales analysis, marketing mix attribution and planning, assortment planning, etc. These can all be transformed with analytics and machine learning. Here, though, we're focusing on what these techniques can do to help you get closer to the individual customer.

In this chapter, we'll frequently employ the term 'use case'. This describes a single specific application of AI. For example, a company might select 'cross-selling product X to high-value customers' and 'increasing retention on the premium support service' as its two initial AI use cases.

Principles for applying analytics

Just as important as the level of analytical power brought to bear is the approach you take in applying it. As we move into the era of AI and machine learning – and see new job roles created, such as 'data scientist' – it's easy to think that the right way to start is to provide the data to mathematical or statistical geeks who will work their magic on it. Two things should be borne in mind:

- This should never be a 'blind' application of technology, throwing data at smart algorithms, even if we hire smart technologists to do the throwing. Analysis should follow a methodological, systematic approach.
- This is not just a technical exercise. It is crucial to incorporate business knowledge. Simply 'throwing data over the wall' to technologists may deliver analyses that are technically good but that miss subtle and important business considerations. Marketers have to either participate hands-on in the analytical work or be part of a closely knit team in which they collaborate with the technical analytical experts on all steps of the project.

And, above all, remember: business imperatives and objectives drive projects, and it's the improvements in business outcomes that are the true measures of success.

AI capabilities – algorithms and models

Models are used to apply AI to marketing. A model receives input data, such as a customer's attributes. It uses this information to produce one or more outputs, such as the product most likely to appeal to the customer, the customer's propensity to respond to a particular offer and so on.

Machine learning algorithms create models, based on their analysis of historical data. These models are updated as customer behaviour and preferences change by re-learning from the latest data available. There are many types of algorithm, but, rather than considering the technical details of these, we're interested in your goals in marketing personalization and what AI can do to help you achieve them. At the heart of that, of course, you want to know about your customers: what segments are there in your market or customer base? And, beyond that, what are the characteristics and profiles that distinguish each customer and let you consider them as individuals? This is the fundamental 'Who?' question. For each of these customers, you need to care about:

- **What** message they would react to? What product will they buy and what content will be most effective in getting them to the point of purchase?
- **How** do they choose to interact with you, i.e. through which set of channels? If what they purchase is a service product, how do they use it? How do they pay for it?
- **When do** they prefer interactions to happen? At what time of day will they be most receptive to a communication from you? In the longer term, when will they move through the different phases of the customer lifecycle and which points in their journey will be most critical for you?

So, the key considerations for AI algorithms and model types are the capabilities they provide and what those mean for you in terms of answering the 'Who?', 'What?', 'How?' and 'When?' questions that can help you to drive a customer-centric business. Following are the main capabilities of AI models and algorithms that can feed directly into your marketing:

- **Classification** lets you distinguish, for example, buyers of a product from non-buyers. You can use this to predict who will (or won't) buy and classification algorithms may also generate profiles – the most distinguishing set of characteristics – for typical buyers and non-buyers.

Mary has the task of coming up with the content for a campaign on the new managed investment product the bank is rolling out. She looks at the classification model built from the test marketing results and two profiles for likely responders immediately catch her eye: one describes older, affluent and conservative customers; the other younger customers whose salary deposits have risen above average over the past three years and who make high-value purchases. She crafts two messages: for the former, she makes it all about security and confidence in steady (and impressive) growth; for the latter, she highlights the innovative investment strategies and potential for high earnings.

- **Scoring** predicts the likelihood of something happening: the likelihood a customer will respond, will buy, will terminate a service, etc. While in some ways this does the same job as classification, having an individual score for each customer or case allows you to make relative decisions, such as ranking customers and making comparisons between them. Take Storytel's use of a 'book score'; many books may be a potential fit for a reader but scoring them allows Storytel to ensure that only the very best matches are suggested.

Call centre agent Sarah has taken a call from an irate subscriber, Simon. As Simon rants about his poor experience with the company and she records the notes, every time she hits <return> Sarah sees Simon's churn score rise; starting from a moderate green 0.35, it quickly becomes an alarming 0.87, highlighted in pulsing red on her screen. She takes a deep breath and prepares to unleash some impressive retention offers.

- **Clustering** or **auto-segmentation** algorithms find the 'natural' groupings of customers for you, and the profiles of these clusters. As you'll read in Chapter 4, Interflora did this with the text people put on greetings cards in order to identify how different types of message imply different occasions; clustering effectively groups together different ways people might phrase messages for the same occasion. Storytel applies it to identify groups that use its service in particular ways – commuters, evening readers, children's book readers and so on. This can be truly transformational in marketing segmentation, and we've devoted a whole section to this below.

- **Association analysis** identifies sets of items that tend to occur together. It is frequently applied to items purchased together, and therefore it is often referred to as 'basket analysis'. It produces rules such as: "When A and B are purchased together, there is a 72% chance that C will also be purchased." You can use this technique as the basis for making cross-selling recommendations. Note that its data foundation isn't limited to products purchased in a single transaction; it can look at all the products a customer has ever bought from you.

Ingrid's team has just received the association analysis of last week's in-store sales. Exploring them, she notices a very strong association: many of the customers who bought two or more of the new vegetable chip range also bought one of the own-brand range of fish and seafood dips. Ingrid knows the systems will automatically use that information to send fish dip coupons to loyalty card holders who recently bought veggie chips. She sends a quick email to the space planners suggesting they display the chips and dips prominently together.

- **Sequence detection** is similar to association analysis but finds sets of items or events that happen in a particular sequence over time. These algorithms can detect patterns that lead to a good outcome (e.g. purchase or upgrade) so you can establish 'shortcuts' to these, or identify paths to bad outcomes (e.g. contract cancellation) and figure out how to avoid them. It can be used in areas such as identifying website visit paths that lead to a purchase, or sequences of events that give early warnings of, say, termination of a service.

  Igor works in the airline's loyalty department. For the first time, the department's analysts have been applying sequence analysis to frequent flyer data. One finding is that Gold Members who have had an upgrade request turned down and then, within a month, have been on two flights with serious delays subsequently show a sudden drop in their spending – presumably choosing to fly with someone else. Igor talks to his boss and convinces him that whenever this pattern is detected they should intervene. An upgrade voucher will immediately be sent to the Gold Member involved. The effect is significant – a measurable increase in retained spend by Gold Members.

- **Forecasting** or **estimation** gives you a predicted numerical value for something that will happen over time – for example, how much a customer will spend on a new service or product, or what their lifetime value will be. This is often combined with other predictions to reach a decision – for example, which of the customers who are likely to accept a credit card upgrade offer would go on to show the most profitable spending. As mentioned above, aggregating these individual estimates can give you an overall projection in the style of traditional 'headline' forecasting, providing KPPs that anticipate future trends in the business (see Chapter 5).

Students get the worst deals and lowest priority service at the bank. Their contribution to revenue and profits is pitiful; why waste time and money pampering them? Then, the customer analytics team introduces a Predictive Customer Value model. The team demonstrates that the model, running against historical data, can accurately estimate customer value up to ten years ahead. Applying it to student account holders, the bank realizes that while many of the students will indeed stay poor in the foreseeable future, others will become extremely profitable customers over a ten-year horizon. Immediately, the bank begins to construct special packages it can offer to students with high predicted future profit.

The actual algorithm used to do a job is often unimportant. They really should be thought of as commodities, rather than any of them being as potential 'silver bullets' whose technical superiority will automatically solve the world's problems (or marketing's at least!). Sometimes, though, particular use cases find aspects of certain algorithms to be especially relevant or useful. To illustrate this, let's look at two characteristics in which algorithms differ – *opacity* (the extent to which the models that algorithms produce are 'black boxes', whose internal workings are hard or impossible to understand) and *granularity* (the degree to which models can differentiate between individual cases).

Neural networks and decision trees can both be used for scoring. Neural networks are based on the operation of the brain, with values propagating through a network of 'neurons'. They are particularly effective in application areas that mimic subconscious human decision-making, such as image process-ing and pattern recognition. They are useful in marketing, though, because they can output a continuous range of scores allowing very fine granularity for differentiating between indi-viduals. Their opacity is sometimes seen as a shortcoming as it's hard to understand precisely how a neural network in the human brain arrives at a decision. The image below depicts a neural network predicting propensity to respond.

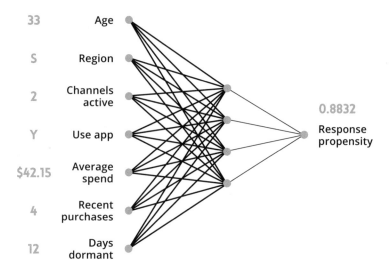

Decision trees are models where decisions are reached by traversing a tree structure. At each branching point, an attrib-ute is tested to determine which branch to follow. Decisions result from arriving at what is called a 'leaf', which specifies an outcome and/or score. Decision trees have the advantage of being relatively easy to read and understand. However, because every case arriving at the same leaf will get the same score, decision trees produce a 'lumpy' distribution of scores without granularity and with no distinction between the cases that have been lumped together.

The image below shows a decision tree that identifies likely responders and non-responders, and also returns an associated score (dotted branches represent deeper sub-trees not included here).

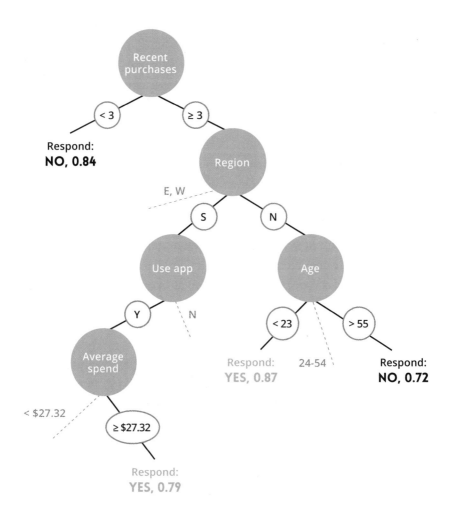

What if you want the best of both worlds? Well, one approach is to use both model types: neural networks (with their fine-grained scoring) to drive optimal campaign execution and decision trees or other rule-based model types (probably trained for classification rather than scoring) to gain an understanding of the factors that determine the likelihood of responding. Other advanced approaches include training a decision tree on the neural network's outputs, rather than on historical response data, in order to extract explanations of how the neural network is making its decisions.

Evaluating performance – 'predicting the past'

How can we be sure that an algorithm has successfully 'learned' and produced a model whose recommendations will be accurate, dependable and valuable? In traditional statistics (remember those stats classes?), it was always assumed the data you were analysing was a very small subset of what could be seen in the world. This meant a lot of effort went into coming up with theoretical measures of confidence to estimate the accuracy and reliability of statistical models. In today's data-rich world, however, where shortage of data is rarely an issue, empirical testing of machine learning models against large and comprehensive sets of data will usually give much more relevant detailed information on their performance.

This stems from what might sound a rather odd capability of predictive models: not only can they predict the future but they can also 'predict' the past. In other words, predictive models can be tested against historical data – unseen by the machine learning algorithm – in what is effectively a 'What if?' simulation. Perhaps you have five years of historical data. You might build your model from the first three years, then test it on the remaining two to see what would have happened had the model been available and in use then.

How many purchases would it have correctly predicted? What proportion of churners would it have identified before they left? And so on. Put the business metrics around this – what increased sales or higher retention would mean in financial terms – and you have a strong business case made before you take the step of operationalizing the analytical recommendations in your marketing.

Understanding insights

As we've already mentioned, some types of model are opaque. Testing their performance to the level where you can be confident of their accuracy is often good enough (how many of us worry about the autopilot that's landing the airliner we're flying in?), but in many cases you'll want to know more about what underlies their decisions. You may want to understand which insights from their 'learnings' can help you understand more about your customers and could inspire you in developing your messaging, content and offers.

This is where machine intelligence and human knowledge come together. From a mass of discovered insights, marketers can identify those most interesting and with the most potential to help drive marketing activities. Human knowledge can also be invaluable in helping to interpret findings that may seem strange, or even counter-intuitive. Several years ago, one of us worked with a business-to-business company that was involved in a project to classify people who were likely and unlikely to respond to a particular biannual marketing campaign. One of the strongest profiles the algorithms discovered for those unlikely to respond was the ones having the property 'Marital Status = UNKNOWN'. Analysts were puzzled and tried to work out what this meant. They speculated that perhaps asking customers for their marital status would upset, annoy and alienate them to the extent that they would no longer respond to offers. However, when the marketing manager was presented with the finding, he quickly understood what was behind it. The company had only started collecting that particular data point three years ago. Since then, in any contact with the customer, such as a call to the service hotline, agents had been prompted to ask for this additional piece of information. So marital status being unknown really meant "we have had no contact with this customer for at least three years" – an indication of disengagement that makes sense in the profile of non-responders. There was no field in the data specifying the time since last contact, but the machine learning algorithms had latched onto this data as a good proxy for that important characteristic.

Understandable insights play an important role in the early stages of analytical adoption; showing potential doubters that algorithms are learning something sensible can help to build their confidence in the technology. Showing that models identify known facts or confirm widely believed hypotheses can boost confidence, but this evidence can still be dismissed by sceptics ("What's the value? It's telling us things we know already!"), and simple findings (e.g. propensity to purchase short-sleeved shirts increases in late spring) can be considered trivial. A good approach is to pick a reasonably complex profile (simple enough to understand but beyond the simple rules of thumb marketers might use to explain behaviour), extract all the data matching that profile and then show unequivocally that (say) the response rate among customers with that profile is much higher than among the overall customer base.

The danger of bias

Human decision-making is often skewed towards particular outcomes in certain cases – a phenomenon known as 'bias'.

Machine learning algorithms learn from data, and, while that data may be expected to be factual and objective, the way in which it is selected and represented may implicitly embody aspects of human bias. This results in the biased opinions of humans being embedded in the models they produce. In areas such as law and employment, poorly designed models may perpetuate race or gender discrimination.

In a marketing context, bias is unlikely to have such dire consequences, but it can still have an impact. We may apply machine learning to data from past campaigns to refine and improve our targeting and see valuable results and high returns from that. But, when it comes down to it, we are limiting the algorithms to learning how to do what we already do, but 'better' (at scale, with greater precision and accuracy). This is also bias; we narrow the algorithms' view, so they consider only the scope of our existing efforts. Models may perpetuate and amplify any flaws in current marketing strategy because the training data is based on what was done, rather than the range of tactics that could potentially work.

What can you do about this? Most importantly, you should be cognizant of the issue – and beware of any data that only perpetuates your current practice. Focusing on your success and trying to fine-tune what you have done before can bring substantial rewards, but might you be missing out on other business opportunities?

A good approach is to be more willing to run experiments and tests. Send offers to a sample of customers who fall outside your standard marketing selection; adding their responses to the data you use to train your AI model lets it learn to include such potential responders in future selections. You can also extend this process to the model's ongoing learning: if you send offers to a sample of customers who were not targeted by the model and include their response data, the model will have the opportunity to learn to correct its false negatives as well as false positives.

Take experimentation as far as you wish. Rather than starting a new offer with standard marketing selections, consider running a test campaign against a random sample of customers – then have AI learn from scratch, bias free, where the campaign works and where it doesn't.

TRANSFORMING MARKETING PRACTICE WITH MACHINE LEARNING – SEGMENTATION

With the wide range of AI and analytical techniques available, how can you use them to meet specific marketing objectives? To get a better understanding, let's look in some depth at a traditional marketing task: segmentation.

Traditional segmentation involves identifying different groups, or segments, that can be distinguished by simple rules about their characteristics or behaviour. The definition of the segments comes from assumptions by marketers, possibly based on high-level and/or qualitative market research.

The problem is that this assumption-based approach provides a 'wishful' segmentation model, rather than one that is necessarily grounded in reality. And, even if it is a 'good' and useful fit, the speed with which consumer behaviour and preferences change in the modern world means not only that individuals frequently drift between segments but also that segment definitions become out of date and fit less and less with reality.

Machine learning enables a data-driven approach that uses clustering algorithms to automatically create segmentation models based objectively on the actual data. For the sake of clarity, we'll refer to this as 'auto-segmentation'. This is the type of clustering undertaken by Martin's team at Storytel in the opening narrative of this chapter.

Clustering algorithms can work from any subset of data. For example, customers might be clustered on their descriptive attributes, on their behaviour or on a combination of the two. Each cluster that the algorithms automatically discover can be considered a segment.

As we saw at Storytel, finding the distinguishing features of these clusters can tell you important things about the people in them and how best to shape your marketing (and indeed your offerings) for each cluster. That information can be identified through cluster-viewing tools, which help to visualize these clusters, or by applying further machine learning algorithms to automatically extract the clusters' profiles. For example, you could create a classification algorithm to tell you the difference(s) between members of 'Cluster 19' and the rest of the population.

It is also analytically straightforward to overlay key metrics on individual clusters. For example, you can easily find which clusters have the highest average propensity to buy a particular category, or the highest average spend, or the lowest loyalty. Analysing these metrics tells you which clusters to target, while their profiles provide ideas and inspiration for the messaging and content that will be most effective for them.

Cluster models built by auto-segmentation are dynamic; they will automatically fit any existing or new customer into the best-matching segment ('tagging' the customers like Storytel does) and will continually re-evaluate existing customers to track their movement between segments. And, very importantly, algorithms can be automated to periodically refresh the cluster model and identify changes in the overall segmentation – so the segmentation is always firmly based on the latest data and up to date with the current characteristics of the customer base.

PREDICTING WHAT WE HAVEN'T BEEN TOLD

In Chapter 2 we talked about collecting data from customers. When you ask customers to submit data – whether providing facts for registration or providing information on their feelings and attitudes in response to a questionnaire – you can never be certain you'll get an answer and, if you do, whether what you get will be the truth, the whole truth and nothing but the truth. What customers tell you isn't always an accurate representation of their intent or behaviours. Information may be omitted, wrong values may be entered in error or a customer may deliberately give you information they know to be inaccurate. Beyond these issues with data quality and completeness, there's also the challenge that when we request data – say, by questionnaire – we usually ask a sample of the customer base, and only a proportion of those supply the requested information. So we can know these small numbers of customers very well, but not those who were never asked or didn't reply.

We've been focusing on how AI can drive better marketing actions, but it's also worth knowing how the machine learning algorithms that create predictive models can help you to address these issues with the data you collect.

Imputing and correcting values

With AI, you can build a predictive model from the data of customers who *did* give you certain information (e.g. their income) that gives a good estimate, based on all the other information provided, for cases where customers did *not* give you that information. And that same model – or its equivalent for any other information that customers tend to omit – can also be used as a validation tool. It can identify cases where the value given is abnormally far from what's predicted, with the option to replace the dubious value.

These predicted values are probabilistic estimates rather than hard deterministic facts. But, with due care taken to test and validate the models that predict them, they will still often be more useful than holes (or glaringly inaccurate entries) in your customer data.

From the few to the many

How can you better use information provided by a relatively small number of respondents more broadly? This is the process you need to follow to leverage this data across your customer base:

- Select a 'target' field – often attitudinal, such as satisfaction level.
- Collate the data from the respondents, but only fields for which there is data for all customers, such as standard behavioural information or elements of descriptive data that are held for all customers.
- Create a model to predict the target.
- Apply that model across the entire customer base.

Cablecom (now UPC) in Switzerland was very successful in understanding customer satisfaction and its drivers among the company's cable TV customers. By surveying customers at key points in the customer lifecycle, and combining their satisfaction levels with other data, Cablecom was able to identify over 100 factors that could predict satisfaction levels for *any* customer with a high degree of accuracy. Based on this, Cablecom used predictive models to identify customers likely to churn and take pre-emptive action. The results were impressive, with a drop in churn rate from 19% to 2% among customers who experienced the pre-emptive action.[28]

FROM DATA TO ANALYSIS TO ACTION

From data to analysis

In Chapter 2 we talked about the collection of data from a wide range of sources. This data is the 'fuel' of analytics, and in most cases will need to be brought into the right 'shape' for analysis to be done effectively. There are two aspects to this: data organization, and data preparation and feature engineering.

Data organization

Most machine learning algorithms work on data that is flattened out into 'tuples', in which a single row represents each case (e.g. customer), with each column representing an attribute. For 'supervised' machine learning, one (or more) of these columns will be a 'target' – for example, a flag indicating whether the customer responded to a particular offer. The exact format and content of records will vary across different use cases. It is common practice to create an 'analytical data view' that brings together and synchronizes all available data; data sets for specific use cases are pulled from this overall analytical data view as required.

Data preparation and feature engineering

Before the machine learning algorithm begins its work, data usually needs to be prepared. This involves mundane issues such as identifying and addressing data quality, or imbalances in the distribution of values that could cause challenges to the algorithms or skew results. Techniques such as over- and under-sampling – effectively telling the algorithms to pay more attention to infrequent outcomes or less to frequent outcomes, respectively – help to ensure algorithms genuinely learn patterns of outcomes which do not occur very often. More interestingly, this is also the stage when data can be enriched and enhanced, in a process often referred to as 'feature engineering'. This involves deriving higher-level features from the basic attributes to potentially give the algorithms more useful information to work from. Some of these derived features might be simple: for example, deriving age from date of birth.

Other richer examples might involve processing whole series of records to derive features that describe how customer behaviour changes over time – for example, looking at how the frequency of customers' purchases or usage level of a service has been trending across the last three, six and twelve months. Or it could be a case of processing images or video clips to extract meaningful features – essentially, a description of what's being 'seen' – that can be used more easily by machine learning algorithms. This takes place at Amazon Go stores, as we saw in Chapter 2.

Doing the analysis – tools and approaches
Who's doing it?
Staffing for analytics will be a key factor in determining which tools and technologies are selected.

Much is made of the 'data scientist' role, which according to a popular *Harvard Business Review* article is "the sexiest job of the 21st century".[29] These are top-end analytics professionals who should be capable of working at any level of technical detail required. But recruit with care: anyone with basic experience of public domain machine learning tools could pitch themselves as a 'data scientist'.

Regardless of the technical calibre of your data scientists, it is important that analysis doesn't become a technical exercise that is separated from the business; close involvement of people with business knowledge is critical for success. For this reason, some companies take the approach of having some of their existing marketing personnel develop analytical skills, or at least the ability to drive the inclusion of advanced analytics in marketing execution.

We've listed below the main options for analytical tooling. Note that if you choose to adopt a customer data platform (see our introduction to these in Chapter 2), it is quite possible that it will incorporate analytical capabilities or tools.

Of course, you might decide to outsource analytical work to a consultancy or an external third party. In that case, you will probably expect them to select the analytical platform and simply deliver the outputs and results to you. Be aware of potential compliance issues with data sharing, though.

Code-level approaches

Today, much analytical work is done in languages such as R and Python. These have the advantage that public domain (open source) implementations are widely available at no or low cost, and many libraries of algorithms and utilities can be accessed easily. The downside is that, as with any programmer-level work, it is labour intensive, and having to concentrate on detailed coding considerations takes the focus away from the objectives and process of analysis. These approaches are for the data scientist; it's unlikely you would want to train your marketing staff to a high level of R programming proficiency.

Visual workbenches

A range of tools are available that take a 'visual programming' approach to advanced analytics. With these systems, users place icons on the screen representing sources of data, ways of manipulating data (e.g. for feature engineering), exploration tools (e.g. visualizations), machine learning algorithms and other utilities; they then connect these to specify analytical 'flows' or processes. Most decent tools of this kind are commercial software and require some investment, but they can benefit a range of users: the best of these tools not only enable non-expert analysts (such as your marketers) to work with advanced algorithms (automatically configured for them) but also provide high productivity (and the opportunity to work at a 'train of thought' level) coupled with detailed technical control for even the most expert analysts. As products with commercial release cycles, they rarely offer access to the latest emerging algorithms as early as users of code-level tools can pick them up from libraries, but most visual workbenches offer the ability to integrate R and/or Python code.

Packaged solutions

The quickest path to initial success can often come from packaged solutions that inject AI into specific marketing activities. For marketing departments not yet ready to build up their own AI and advanced analytics skills, they can be a quick way to prove the value of AI for boosting marketing returns in specific areas – for example, intelligently targeting follow-ups to abandoned baskets, or sending repurchase reminders based on learning individual customers' replenishment cycles. While everybody loves quick wins, you need to make sure that the solution you're acquiring isn't going to leave you confined to simple, packaged analyses. You must also ensure that you have a path to expand beyond the packaged solution to build up and apply your own AI capabilities once you've proved their value.

Automating for scale

Whatever approach you take, the ability to carry out one-off analyses only takes you so far. A marketing organization fully enabled with AI will be applying many predictive models across its operations; the higher the level of granularity and individuality required, the more models, considering more facets of customer behaviour and preference, will be needed. As the number of models grows, so does the task of monitoring their performance and updating them so their recommendations and decisions stay current and relevant as preferences and behaviour change.

These requirements rapidly exceed the capacity of manual analysis. To be successful at a true one-to-one level of personalization and keep the machine intelligence up to date with a dynamic and volatile customer base, analytical processes need to be packaged and run automatically, at scale, without human intervention. Once an organization has taken this step from hand-crafted analysis to an 'analytical factory', you can be confident in your ability to expand your application of AI to any size of customer base.

From analysis to action

No matter how perfect and complete your data might be, or how wonderfully accurate your predictive models are, none of this will produce value until you carry it through into marketing execution and action.

Some of these actions will be based on machine intelligence enabling human decisions makers to do their job better – for example, prompting with predictive information derived from data in the CRM software for better customer service. In the same way that AI needs automation to scale its intelligence, you can only deliver the full benefit if the execution based on that intelligence is equally automated and capable of working to the same level of granularity.

Sometimes, you will need to think carefully about how to apply your predictive models to take account of differences between your customers. As we noted in Chapter 2, data collection from customers is often incremental, and this means you will see different degrees of data completeness for different customers. Limiting predictive models to only consider the subset of data that is universal to all customers would result in missing out on getting better predictive performance on those you know more about. Thankfully, as specific data tends to be collected at specific points in the lifecycle, it is likely there will be several discrete levels of completeness in your customer base. You might therefore separate out groups based on data completeness levels and build a model for each. Then, when you put that into action, the best model is chosen for each customer based on how complete their data is.

In the next chapter, we'll tell you about the relevant communications and personalized service experiences you can drive as you move from analysis to action.

OPTIMIZATION

Using predictive models helps you to increase the chance of success of each client interaction; for each customer and opportunity, using insight and foresight will help to ensure you make the right decision. By working in this way – considering every interaction independently – you can think of what you're aiming for as the 'set of best decisions'.

Optimization techniques help you to achieve the 'best set of decisions', where the entire set of decisions – in this case, customer interactions – is considered as a whole to maximize the total value or benefit that can be obtained.

Applied to marketing campaigns and interactions, optimization takes into account the predicted behaviour of each individual customer (their propensity to respond to a variety of offers or messages, their likely spend, their channel preference, etc.), parameters such as the cost of different types of interaction, constraints such as channel capacity and overall budget, and objectives such as maximizing response or revenue. A mathematical optimization engine runs across this whole scenario and returns a plan – effectively the right offer or interaction for each customer – that will work within the constraints and give the best overall result in terms of meeting the objective.

By using predictive analytics combined with an optimization approach to drive its campaigns, Banco Itaú Argentina, operating in a highly competitive market, saw revenue from existing clients rise by 40% and increased its total retail customer contribution margin by close to 60%.[30]

BEYOND SELLING –
NEXT BEST ACTION

Although in marketing our actions are usually offers or other encouragements to buy, organizations that are savvy about building long-term value in customer relationships often talk about a 'next best action' (NBA) approach rather than a 'next best offer'. This is what Martin's team from Storytel was working towards at the start of this chapter.

At any point in the customer relationship, there may be a number of actions that could be taken towards the customer. Some of these will undoubtedly be offers. Other actions, though, don't focus on generating revenue directly: they could be an apology and compensation for something that the customer complained about, or a pre-emptive change to a tariff that generates lower revenue in the immediate term but boosts loyalty and potential customer lifetime value, or free training, guidance or information that helps customers to get more out of a product they've bought, and so on.

Deciding, among all those offers and other actions, what is the best action to take at a given point in time or interaction will depend on multiple factors, many of them the output of predictive models, such as:
- propensities to buy various products (categories, upgrades, add-ons, etc.)
- susceptibility to current and forthcoming offers and campaigns
- retention risk
- predicted satisfaction levels (and causal factors)
- current and estimated future value.

Applying the NBA successfully requires an automated process to scale the following approach to every interaction with
every customer:

- Get up-to-date scores from predictive models (either from
  the latest scheduled run of the models or from an on-
  demand run).
- Use business rules that work across propensity scores and
  other insights and come up with potential actions and recommendations.
- In an arbitration step, evaluate and rank these potential
  actions, and select the best.
- Execute the best action.

As with any application of advanced analytics, a 'closed loop'
is needed; the success of actions is monitored, rules and arbitration criteria are fine-tuned and the models are continually
updated from the latest data as consumer behaviour changes.

WHERE DO YOU START?

We've taken you through the ways AI can contribute to your
marketing efforts, and we hope your brain is bubbling over
with possibilities. But you're probably thinking, "So where do
I start?"

There's no single answer to this question; the right starting
point could be different for every organization. Here we'll
give you some thoughts on what factors to consider in choosing your starting point and in planning your AI 'journey'
beyond that.

Pick the low-hanging fruit

Everyone wants quick wins, especially when new initiatives are involved. In such cases it is important to show value quickly and reassure peers and management (and yourself!) that AI and advanced analytics are good things with genuine benefit to the organization.

A good starting point is to list the use cases where you could apply AI in your business. Then, for each of these, consider the following factors.

How does it fit with the marketing objectives?

If your business's focus is entirely on customer acquisition, retention and churn management may not be the best place to start.

Does it add value?

Short of trying this out in-house, one of the best ways to become confident is to consider what has worked for competitors or other businesses like yours. Seek out case studies and look to follow well-trodden paths where others have been successful.

What value is it likely to bring?

Try to put a number on what each use case could mean to you. If predictive targeting of a particular offer type tripled the response rate, what would that mean? If cross-sell offers during online shopping increased basket size by 10%, how much would that be worth? Consider optimistic, pessimistic and likely scenarios.

How demanding is the analytical approach?

More complex projects will take longer, require more skills and implicitly carry higher risk.

What data is required?

Projects with simple data requirements will be easier to run than cases where you have to embark on additional data collection or have to pre-process the data extensively.

How easily can the results be operationalized?

Remember, no analytics project delivers value until its results are carried through to action. Consider how much effort it will take to fit the analytical outputs into existing operations; the cases where they can slot seamlessly into existing systems and processes, with little or no reworking of these, will be good starting points.

Next, rank your portfolio of possible use cases according to these criteria and select the best place(s) to start. If this process sounds daunting, don't worry too much. Despite the number of criteria involved, it will usually quickly become clear that no matter how big the set of possible projects you list, there are only at most a small handful of prime starting points. And you don't have to do this yourselves; product, service and consultancy vendors with experience in this area will be keen help to you.

While we can't tell you that "This is where you should start!", it's clear that some types of application will usually be more natural starting points than others. Take, for example, purchase-based product cross-sell. This uses easily accessible (association) algorithms and in its simplest form it requires only purchase data. Many companies have done this to great effect. Using it to follow up recent purchases by sending personal emails with recommendations should be relatively straightforward and the value delivered should be easy to measure through response to these recommendations. By contrast, a full NBA implementation is unlikely to be anyone's first step. It requires a range of predictive models to be created and managed, which requires a range of data sources. However, relatively few companies can claim to have developed a comprehensive NBA system as it requires integration with operational systems across all channels, with the ability to operate in real time. While the potential benefits may be huge, quantifying this value requires the potentially complex measurement of incremental customer lifetime value.

Is there enough data?

This has to be one of the most commonly asked questions by people looking at adopting AI and advanced analytics. It comes down to two concerns.

Is the data (i.e. my business) big enough?

Almost certainly, yes! If your customers number in the hundreds rather than the thousands, tens of thousands or millions, the incremental value you can obtain with these techniques may be marginal. But, if what you are providing for your small number of customers is a valuable service rich in data-generating interactions, these techniques may still be well worth considering.

There is no magic number of cases above which data is 'sufficient'. We have seen successful applications of predictive technology with only a few hundred records, and cases where, despite millions of records being available, no reliable models could be built as little of the data was meaningful.

How do I start when the data is incomplete or imperfect?

One of the biggest obstacles to the adoption of AI and advanced analytics is the paralysis companies suffer when they delay until their data is ready. A true 360-degree view is an aspiration, not something that can ever realistically be achieved, and few, if any, companies can claim 100% data quality.

Managing data is a cost; the sooner you can liberate value by analysing it, the better.

The reality is that AI and advanced analytics techniques cope well with data that may have quality issues. And, in terms of completeness of data, that's one factor to consider in the selection of 'low-hanging fruit' (described above). Many use cases can work initially with limited data, with the addition of more data over time increasing the accuracy of the models involved and the value delivered. Start pragmatically with the readily available data, and with the right analytical tools you can add more data sources as they become available. This will require little or no change to the analytical processes you have already created.

The journey

The process you go through to assess possible use cases can be the basis of your road map for rolling out advanced analytics and AI across an organization. You create a series of potential projects as the steps on your journey. Each delivers incremental value in its own right, and, as you undertake each project, you are progressively building up both your capabilities and your infrastructure. This means that, as you progress to more substantial and demanding projects, not only are you better equipped to tackle them but also the time, effort and cost involved are lower than they would have been at the start of your journey thanks to the advances you have already made.

The same applies to your data. Aim to develop your data assets, and improve their quality, incrementally. This enables use cases with more substantial data requirements, and additionally the new data sources that become available can feed into upgrading the analyses you've already tackled and lift the value you obtain from them.

LOOKING TO THE FUTURE

AI is a rapidly developing technology area; some developments that are considered the future for most organizations are already in use by pioneering adopters and proving their value today.

"In the beginning was the word …"

Many organizations have progressed to incorporating unstructured data in the form of text in their customer analyses. Natural language processing (NLP) techniques pick up certain topics or 'concepts' that customers mention – for example, in call centre conversations – and that give clues to their interests and preferences. Some companies are going further, using sentiment analysis techniques to understand the feelings and emotions behind a customer's words.

Storytel's use of NLP is innovative and reflects its unique position as a text-rich business. By directly analysing the content of books, the company gains a more powerful ability to match them to readers than can be gained from the simple metadata that describes a book. This approach is not restricted to companies dealing with literature. By combining response data with analysis of the text of communications, many marketing operations could use this approach to discover exactly which elements of content lead to the best customer engagement.

Going deep

At the time of writing this book, deep learning is one of the AI approaches that is generating the most excitement and hype.

Deep learning algorithms are particularly powerful in 'sub-symbolic' applications, such as recognizing content in images and videos. While some organizations have begun to apply them in marketing, the application areas we've described in this book are usually tackled effectively by using more traditional machine learning techniques.

Can deep learning make a valuable contribution to marketing? Absolutely, especially as marketers begin to work with unstructured data beyond text. The Swiss company NVISO provides solutions that instantaneously measure the emotional reactions of consumers. This is done, with the consent of the user, in real time using standard camera devices installed on everyday products, such as phones, tablets and computers. Imagine being able to record consumers' reactions to the content you show and have that, along with all the other data you hold, help to make your AI models even more accurate in predicting preferences.

Bots, bots, bots

Bots are popping up everywhere, keen to chat with you whether you are a casual browser visiting a shopping site for the first time or a bank customer being offered advice on your financial holdings.

Currently, we see two main directions for bots. First, a lot of work is going into making bots as lifelike as possible in their conversations. Whole new jobs are coming into existence to 'educate' bots, with these jobs staffed not by data scientists or AI geeks but people with training in languages, communication and psychology. The famous Turing Test – can you tell whether it's a human or a computer on the other end of the line? – is suddenly hugely relevant; can users spot the transition from being handled by a low-cost bot to being handled by an expensive human agent? The further bots can go while continuing to appear human-like – in terms of both conversation characteristics and the 'quality' of what they communicate – the more flexibility companies will have to support interactive conversational channels while saving the skilled human agents for the most crucial parts of the most important conversations.

Second, even though bot conversations may still be relatively unsophisticated and shallow, we're seeing more and more AI horsepower being put behind them. The North Face has used IBM's Watson cognitive system to power its Expert Personal Shopper (XPS).[31] XPS asks you what you'll be doing, where and when. From that, it anticipates likely weather conditions, takes into account your activity, narrows down the possible range of suitable products, then engages in further dialogue to understand more about your preferences and guide you to the ideal jacket.

APPLYING AI ACROSS THE CUSTOMER EXPERIENCE – SMART JOURNEYS FOR THE BUSINESS TRAVELLER

In this chapter, we have only scratched the surface of what AI can do to help you in your efforts to delight your customers and enhance your relationship with them. We'd like to leave you with a case study that shows how customer interactions needn't be restricted to marketing activities, and how AI can include more than customer data in your customer interactions.

Carlson Wagonlit Travel (CWT), one of the world's leading travel management companies, helps organizations of all sizes to deliver a travel programme that engages employees, empowers them to be more productive and takes complexity out of their on-the-road experience.

CWT's operations are all about finding the optimal balance between the needs of three 'customers':
- **The companies for whom CWT provides travel services**: to manage their costs and ensure compliance with travel policy.
- **The airlines, hotels, etc**: to sell their flights, rooms, etc.
- **The traveller**: to make everything about their travel booking and management experience (and potentially the travelling itself) relevant, easy and frictionless.

Supported by a battery of AI capabilities, CWT weaves these requirements through the entire business travel experience. Within a personalized booking portal, flight and hotel recommendations – effectively sales offers – are based on each traveller's previous behaviour and anticipated preferences. They are therefore highly relevant while always consistent with the employer's travel policies. As well as facilitating every step in each traveller's journey, CWT gives suggestions for where travellers can go or what they can do in their leisure time, which helps to make the relationship more human. And the use of external data on weather, potential aircraft issues, etc. to predict potential travel disruption adds another dimension to the relationship; the traveller knows CWT is watching over them and is not only anticipating but also pre-emptively addressing – by having alternative flight options ready – possible issues or problems.

In this type of integrated end-to-end experience, while AI may be the brains behind the scenes, a lot more than machine intelligence goes into providing communications and services to customers in an effective and relevant way. In the next chapter, we'll tell you all about what's needed to achieve that.

MATURITY IN DATA ANALYTICS & AI

As this chapter has hopefully made clear, gaining value from analysing data depends on a lot more than just the power or complexity of the algorithms you apply. So, what represents maturity in the use of data analytics and AI?

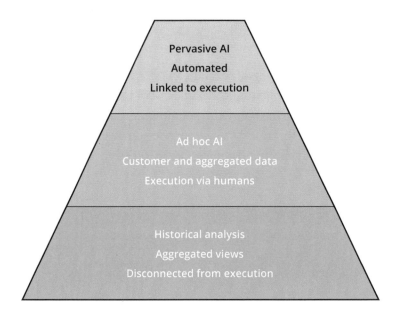

Highest maturity level

Organizations that are mature in their use of AI apply it systematically across their operations. They hold rich, holistic data at individual customer levels, often with the ability to integrate data from multiple departments. They have an infrastructure in which analytical tasks and decision-making processes are automated and linked directly to communication and service execution.

Middle maturity level

Mid-stage organizations apply AI and advanced analytics to their marketing, but in an ad hoc manner. Their analysis is focused around the customer and uses marketing and sales data, much of it held at the individual level but with some elements only available in aggregate form (e.g. anonymized surveys, hence mixed-level data). There is a relatively loose connection between analysis and execution; decisions leverage analytical insights but are largely dependent on human-driven steps.

Lowest maturity level

At the lowest maturity level, analyses used in the business are backward looking, mainly consisting of aggregated metrics. The focus is typically across business operations – product sales, operations, etc. – with no customer analysis below the aggregate level. Decisions are based on human viewpoints and assumptions, and there is no connection as such between data, analysis and execution.

Remember that you can take our test based on the Omnichannel Hexagon and find your company's omnichannel maturity level at:

OMNICHANNELFORBUSINESS.ORG

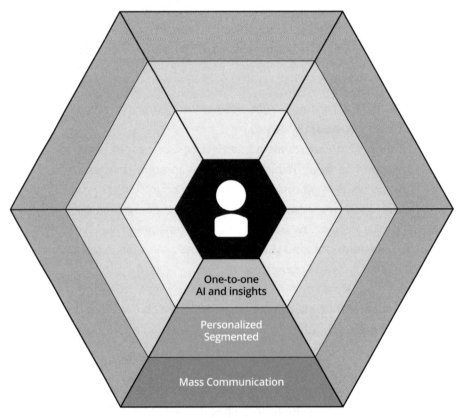

One-to-one
AI and insights

Personalized
Segmented

Mass Communication

COMMUNICATION & SERVICE

4

COMMUNICATION & SERVICE

Data and the insights derived from data by AI have no value until they're put to use. Data and machine intelligence should be used to tailor the right communication, service and deals at the right times. In this way, you will implicitly and explicitly be acknowledging your history with each and every customer, both when you turn to your customers and when they turn to you.

Alex enjoys hiking. Although he's studying business administration at Columbia University in New York, he spends most of his free time either thinking about hiking or enjoying the fresh air of the mountains.

Over the years he has signed up for multiple newsletters from both retailers and brands. None of the newsletters impress him much. Products, products, discount, sale ...

In the summer, Alex finds himself on a trip to San Francisco, where he visits The North Face store. The sales associate tells him about the local trails and recommends a trip to Slacker's Hill. They also talk about The North Face's rewards programme, VIPeak, and Alex signs up for it.

The rewards programme offers an app with loads of interesting content about hiking and inspiration for new destinations and experiences. The sales associate reminds Alex to use the app to check in when he reaches the top of Slacker's Hill.

When Alex reaches the top, he opens The North Face app and checks in at Golden Gate National Recreation Area. Immediately he gets a notification saying he's earned 50 points.

In the following months Alex notices a change in the communications he receives from The North Face. Receiving a "Back to Campus" campaign at just the right time – and containing just the right backpack – makes him think that it's almost as if the company has figured out who he is and what he's interested in. Thinking back, he actually gave them all the clues – the stuff he bought, the places he checked in, his address, what he browsed on the website and what he clicked in the emails. He's just not used to brands keeping their promise to send relevant information to each customer. It brings a small smile to his face and he adds the backpack to his online shopping basket.

COMMUNICATION AND SERVICE

This is how a story from a customer of The North Face in the US might sound. Imagine if you could create such an experience for a large proportion of your customers.

To better understand its customers, The North Face launched a loyalty programme called VIPeak in 2012. As in traditional rewards programmes, points are obtained for every product that is bought, but it doesn't stop there. In line with its brand, The North Face has made it possible to obtain points by 'checking in' through its app to outdoor locations worthy of exploration or by participating in The North Face events. This motivates customers to keep exploring. Loyalty points can be used not only to get reward vouchers for use on future purchases but also for experience-related rewards that are 'on brand', such as rock-climbing or even a trip to Mount Everest base camp if you are a really skilled shopper and/or explorer. Consider which benefits that aren't all about points and discounts that you could offer your customers – make those benefits support your brand and the mission you're on.

Rewards are one thing – relevance is another. You should employ personalization techniques in much the same way as The North Face does. The techniques here are based on simple business rules as well as advanced predictive analytics and AI. For instance, because the school semesters start at different times throughout the US, the timing of the "Back to School" campaign is accommodated to the physical address of members through a simple rule in the campaign. At the other end of the scale, an advanced algorithm analyses the combined data stream for each customer and determines which outdoor disciplines each one is particularly interested in. For one product launch – the Ventrix Jacket – the promotional video was even edited into multiple versions accommodating each discipline and sent to only the members matching those disciplines. According to Ian Dewar, director of customer lifecycle management and analytics at The North Face, the results have been impressive – at a conference in Sweden in August 2018, he presented to the audience that same-year visits in the store for customers receiving this personalized and timely communication are up to three times higher and average transactions are 20% larger than for the average customer. And on top of this come the long-term brand equity benefits of communicating more relevant content instead of just pushing products.

THE FOURTH DISCIPLINE IN OMNICHANNEL MARKETING

In this chapter, we will first discuss what it means for your customers' experience when you succeed in doing omnichannel marketing and which major challenges you will need to overcome in order to achieve this. We will then look closer at the difference between being company-centric and being customer-centric in your marketing. With concrete examples, we'll look into which moments in the customer journey can be leveraged to get closer to customers. We'll use the retail and subscription sectors to exemplify this. Even though timing is essential for coming across as relevant, it's far from being the only tactic. We'll explore other tactics that you can use when you want a message to be experienced as close and relevant to customers and look at which data you can use to achieve this. Realizing that omnichannel plays a special role within retail, we'll introduce the classical omnichannel commerce features that retailers can expect consumers almost to take for granted and how data can be used in-store to further strengthen the customer relationship.

Then we'll discuss how you walk the thin line of using data to be personal and relevant without coming across as creepy. There are certain simple rules to follow to avoid falling into that trap.

Even if the starting point is not about the channels, they will still be important when you want to reach out to your customers. Therefore, we'll discuss what distinguishes the individual channels, so you can decide which channels are relevant to you. How do they differ in their capacity for targeting messages? Are they primarily suitable for push-based or pull-based communication? Are they linked to the rest of your customer data?

System support will be an important parameter when we talk about the need for your company to develop its own media. What types of systems are needed to support insight-based one-to-one communication?

Finally, we will discuss and characterize the different degrees of maturity within the work of using data and insight in communication and service.

FROM 'VICTIM OF A CAMPAIGN' TO 'PROTAGONIST OF THE BRAND'S STORY'

No one likes being sold to, but we all like buying into something, and there is always something we are looking for – after all, we are consumers. We have money, and we'll certainly see that it is used.

That is why mass communication works. When you reach out widely enough, some of the people who are passively watching TV are bound to think that your advertising touches directly on their needs. If you are lucky, some viewers will order the product immediately.

The problem is that there are increasingly few people who have that good feeling. Although the media agency has promised you exposure to specific audiences who are expected to see this specific TV broadcast, the majority of your exposures – and thus your advertising funds – are wasted. The majority of potential customers are at best indifferent to your message; the rest might almost feel like victims of your campaign.

Marketing becomes service

That is why you should work at using insights and data to a greater extent in your communications. It may not always be possible, but when it *is* possible, do it, preferably on media you control. In that way, you can make your personalized offer – i.e. what used to be called marketing – increasingly be perceived as a service rather than an attempt at pushing a sale through.

Service becomes marketing

The case can also be quite the reverse, in the sense that your communications do not have to focus on the right offer at the right time but instead should really be crafted into the appropriate service message that will be seen as value-adding for the customer, without intending to sell anything. This is also why many organizations that focus on building customer relationships refer to the 'next best action' rather than the 'next best offer' (see Chapter 3 for more on this).

For example, in the case of The North Face, when they have sufficient data on members, they take great care to communicate less about the products and more about outdoor experiences they believe the member would enjoy.

Relevance doesn't come overnight

Unfortunately, it is difficult or even impossible to be relevant to all customers all the time.

Working towards relevance in your communications and service is a long and probably never-ending process. It requires customer recognition, data collection and the generation of insights. And, as we'll discuss further in this chapter, it requires the production of an array of creative content elements to suit each customer type. It's a gradual process because you won't have rich contextual data for every customer – not to mention the fact that you won't have all potential customers in your database in the first place.

So maximizing relevance is a game of setting up automated data captures, analytics and automated communication that gradually more and more of your customers will experience. But you still have to do all the marketing that you used to do – all the campaigns, all the paid media, all the mass marketing.

And, of course, you can use data intelligently to target the right audiences and personalize the messaging in the campaigns, but it takes extra effort.

The short version

As the Omnichannel Hexagon suggests for this discipline, the starting point for Communication & Service is mass marketing. If you don't have any (or you have too few) customers in your database, then you have to start with mass marketing in paid media. As you gradually build up sales and scale your marketing permission base, you can incrementally move more of your campaign-based communication into owned media. That's the first measure of success – owned media is generally a lot cheaper than paid media. Data and AI-derived insights can be used to personalize and optimize your campaigns, with different content used to engage different parts of your customer base.

The next step, as illustrated in the central part of this discipline in the omnichannel hexagon, is for AI to help inform the timing of *when* you reach out to customers – this covers not only the time of day but also when is most appropriate in the individual customer lifecycle. Data will not only help you decide what you *should* communicate but also *when* to communicate it. In fact, studies[32] show that using data to find the right moment is often more effective than personalizing the contents of a campaign. This is where the combination of AI and automation comes in. The timing of certain events is unique to every customer, such as when they are most receptive to marketing, when their recurring cycles of behaviour (such as repeat 'replenishment' purchases) fall and when they hit key points in the customer lifecycle.

If you let AI learn these cycles and set up automated communications that are triggered as soon as a customer hits one of those key moments, then you'll have optimized the timing for each customer.

After having launched several flows of automated communication, it is time to establish a continuous process of optimizing what you've built. Put in place ongoing ways of questioning your content, timing and algorithms, and experiment with creative messaging and additional personalization. In this way, you will see a further increase in effect.

COMPANY-CENTRIC VS. CUSTOMER-CENTRIC

For many companies, marketing campaigns follow the production cycle. And quite often the production cycle follows the four seasons. This is not wrong, and it does help to increase relevance that autumn-related products are marketed in the autumn. On top of the seasonal track you'll have the yearly blockbuster occasions, such as Valentine's Day, Mother's Day, Singles' Day (Asia), Black Friday and Christmas. Retailers will also do campaigns on behalf of their suppliers – in essence, suppliers will pay retailers to market specific products at specific times in accordance with *their* campaign plans. You could argue that this is a place where the business model flips around – you selling your customers to your suppliers as opposed to selling the products of your suppliers to your customers.

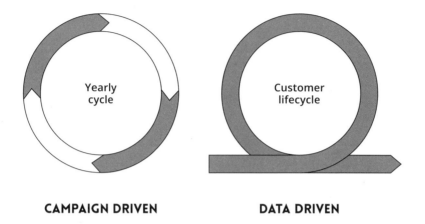

CAMPAIGN DRIVEN   **DATA DRIVEN**

These tactics are all company-centric and follow a campaign mindset. You know the date is coming and prepare the best campaign possible across paid and owned media. Hopefully you are using data where you have it to select the right audiences in paid media and to personalize the message to each customer in owned media. But how about customer-centric communications – where do they fit in? For example, isn't it customer-centric to personalize by gender? Well, it's better than nothing – but you can get closer to a customer than that. Instead of timing your communications in accordance with the yearly cycle, you can time them according to each customer's lifecycle. Throughout their lifecycle, customers will have different considerations on their mind – should they buy 'product A', cancel their subscription or perhaps refer a friend? A data driven approach (see Chapter 2 and 3) can reveal what these things might be and at what point in time a certain customer may be having these considerations. Given this insight, the skilled marketer can then send a message that fits each moment of truth. This of course needs to be automated and data-driven as no human can effectively schedule send-outs for each individual customer in a large database.

How Interflora gets the timing right

Interflora is a flower delivery network that enables customers to send flowers to friends, family and loved ones in most parts of the world. Interflora naturally taps into the blockbuster occasions by reminding people to buy flowers. But, to be honest, everybody can sell flowers on the day before Mother's Day.

The real challenge is to sell flowers on an anonymous and rainy Tuesday afternoon in November, or any other day that doesn't fit the blockbuster occasions. In order to do that, you'd need to know who has a birthday – and, even better, who could be in the market for buying them flowers (or wine, specialties, etc). To get the timing right, Interflora in Denmark first tried asking people to type in their private occasions, such as anniversaries and the birthdays of their friends. For the customers who actually do get around to this and submit their private occasions, the reminders work extremely well. Interflora uses every occasion to motivate customers to submit these private occasions, but, as you can imagine, it is quite hard to make people provide the data. Interflora had to find another solution that could give the same results but at a greater scale (in terms of reaching more customers), so it turned to AI.

While Interflora could mine data from products and transactions, it appears it has more valuable data that comes significantly closer to the feelings involved when sending someone flowers – the greetings card! When you send flowers using Interflora, you can type in the greeting that you want the receiver to get along with the flowers. Interflora has created an AI algorithm that reads the card text and determines with great accuracy the occasion, the intent and the relationship between the buyer and the receiver. So, for example, if a woman sends a man a wine gift on a specific day, the same woman gets a subtle reminder around the same time as last year's purchase. "Do you know anyone who has a birthday soon?" It turns out that Interflora is 95% sure this woman does, and it suggests she buys something that a man may appreciate, such as candy or red wine. This also enables Interflora to send a steady flow of communication reaching a large part of its customer base with the right timing. So, let's have a look at what *the right timing* could be for a few classic business models.

How retail and subscription businesses get the timing right

The customer lifecycle can be simplified by dividing it into three overall phases: Attract, Grow and Retain. In the Attract phase, you know very little about your customer. You use browsing and engagement data to identify what this customer could be interested in and the possible best times to contact them regarding this. Once you have a customer relationship, the Grow phase starts. In this phase, you want to make the customer relationship as deep as possible, maximizing both the profitability and the satisfaction of the customer. In this phase you tend to have much more data at your disposal and thus it should be easier to provide relevant communication. In the Retain phase, the customer is showing signs of leaving you. Often the signs are that you have fewer data points than normal – i.e. you still have their transactions, but it's been a while since the last one and perhaps they aren't opening emails any more. That could very well be a sign that you are going to lose this customer if you don't act.

The image below provides an overview of typical moments in the customer lifecycle that can be tapped into by retailers. Later on in this section, you will find the same image showing these moments for subscription-based businesses. The images are by no means exhaustive in the moments they include, but they should provide inspiration to get your imagination going.

Bear in mind too that there are many moments listed in these images that may also apply to similar sectors or lines of business. Retail and pureplay e-commerce are very similar to travel and other services that can be sold online. Subscription businesses encompass both pure digital services (such as Netflix, HBO and Spotify) and more traditional print magazines and newspapers allowing their customers a subscription. The word 'subscription' could also apply to membership organizations, such as workers' unions, non-governmental organizations and charities, fitness clubs and insurance. In fact, there is a growing trend within retail to offer subscription-based services. Take a look at JustFab.com as an example, or Amazon's 'Subscribe and Save' service. Here you have both retail and subscription in one.

Below are details on each of the moments in retail and subscription-based businesses.

Retail

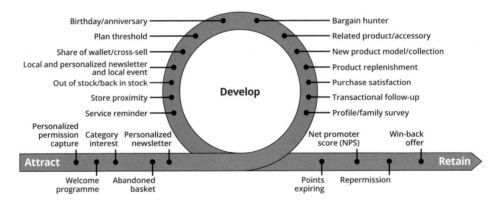

Attract

Personalized permission capture (or sign-up) involves getting consent for communicating directly with the customer (more about this in Chapter 1). Should the customer leave your website or your store, then you have the chance to restart the conversation using owned media. Using immediately accessible online data, it's possible to personalize the bait in the permission prompt. Which competition, discount, product category or gender should be emphasized in the offer? It may be obvious from the data, or scoring models could choose these for you.

This is not an online-only tactic. It can and should be applied to physical touchpoints as well. Make sure to use in-store signage, flyers, stickers in changing rooms and notes on the wrapping and packaging of products to ask for marketing permission.

A **welcome programme** is your chance to give something back to the customers who chose to sign up for your communication. Use this chance to say more about your business and confirm that the customer did the right thing. What's the story behind your business? What's the concept? What can they expect? What kinds of services do you offer, and which of these did the customer perhaps not know about already? To incentivize the first purchase, spice it up with a voucher or something similar – perhaps chosen by an AI model that has learned from what worked for similar newcomers.

Category interest is a moment that relies on the web browsing history of each customer. If data implies that a customer has a particular interest in a certain product category, then make sure to tell all the great stories that you have about this category. It could be small pieces of information about the designer and the thoughts behind the category, or inspiration for how you'd use the products. In the case of The North Face, if a customer has browsed rock-climbing products intensively, provide more information about how they can get great rock-climbing experiences. Again, depending on how aggressive and salesy you wish to be, this can always be spiced up with discounts and personal vouchers. As in most interactions, AI can provide you with more details in terms of knowing exactly which category information is most likely to appeal to this customer.

Abandoned basket is by far the most common moment that every retailer wants to pursue with timely communication. The customer has left a product in the shopping bag but hasn't completed checkout. There are multiple ways of addressing this – you could choose a convenience approach here and say that you've reserved the contents of the basket for a given period of time. You could also suggest alternative products or even try your luck with discount vouchers. However, don't be tempted to give everybody a discount all the time – instead, look into your data and see what is the best option for each individual customer. AI can tell you which abandoned baskets have the best chance of being (with a nudge) resumed and completed, and which might require discounting to tip them into conversion.

A side note to this moment is to incorporate in-store shopping baskets in the data capture for this moment. If you are selling high-value items and the customer cannot quite make up their mind, you should consider saving the shopping basket to an online profile so you can remind the customer later on. The Nordic furniture retailer Bolia is using this tactic with great success.

Variants on abandoned basket tactics include looking for products on people's wishlists or motivating people to complete a sign up. If someone has spent a lot of time online researching a new car or kitchen, or if someone has used advanced app features such as augmented reality visualization of new furniture in their home, these are all moments that can and should be used to continue the conversation towards a likely purchase.

Personalized newsletter is probably the most common communication in the customer lifecycle. AI can recommend which content and offers to include in order to turn a one-size-fits-all newsletter into a personalized communication. If the customer chooses to interact with your newsletter, this can give you important clues as to what the customer is interested in. Make sure you capture the data and follow up with more information on what the customer seems interested in.

Develop

Profile/family survey can actually take place at any point in the customer journey. It's your way as a retailer of encouraging the customer to tell you a bit about themselves and give you the opportunity to become more relevant in the future. Ask about their interests, family relationships (such as kids), clothing sizes, preferences, birthdays and other special days, such as anniversaries. Also keep in mind that this does not have to be an online-only exercise. A visit to a physical store is often a great opportunity to get to know your customer better, and this tactic is applied by brands such as SuitSupply.com and TheTrunkClub.com that combine physical showrooms / stores with e-commerce. As described in Chapter 3, when customers don't provide all the requested information, AI may be able to help fill in some of the blanks.

Transactional follow-up is not to be confused with the order confirmation. But the moment a customer receives an item they've bought, this could be an excuse for reaching out again, possibly to confirm they've made the right choice or to make sure they have all the information they need to get the most out of their purchase. If it's a complicated product, make sure they get the information on how to use it. If it's a design item, you could confirm their purchase decision and provide them with small facts they could use as conversation pieces and help them to become ambassadors for the brand. Again, you can choose to be more salesy and suggest products that belong to the same series or within the same category (or which an association model predicts may also appeal). For example, if someone bought running shoes, you might suggest they now buy socks and tights.

Purchase satisfaction should automatically be prompted shortly after the purchase has been made. Ask separately how the buying experience was and how the product experience is. If the customer is positive, then you can suggest they recommend you as a retailer, give the product a review or perhaps supply you with user-generated content for further marketing of the product. AI and advanced analytics can be used to find patterns of common factors that drive low or high satisfaction.

Product replenishment is a tactic that looks at products that are, or could become, frequently purchased. Typically, these products are those that are consumed, such as body lotion, shampoo, shoes and jeans. You can either do this using rules – reaching out at the timing that in your opinion would fit the most people for each product – or use AI to help determine the optimal timing for each customer and product. If there's a high chance of repurchase at a particular point in time, then trigger an appropriate communication to the customer and make sure it's clear in your creative messaging that you are trying to help them not to run out of their favourites.

New product model/collection is the moment a new model of an existing product is launched. A good example is running shoes. Most running shoes are relaunched every year, for instance the ASICS Kayano. At the time of writing, we're at model number 25. Make sure people who bought the old version are told all the benefits of the new model and perhaps even guide them to how they can sell their old item second hand.

Related product/accessory is similar to 'new product model/ collection', but instead of a new model you should be keeping an eye on new products within a series, a collection or a category. This works best for design products and products such as kitchenware. This tactic can also be used within media, where you can keep an eye out for new books, movies or similar from the same author, producer or series. AI can identify the customers who are most likely to expand their purchasing within the same family of products.

Bargain hunter is not so much about the product as it is about getting a good deal. A cross between the two is ideal, of course. You can use AI algorithms to determine who is especially interested in getting a good deal, and even what level of discount is likely to be a 'trigger' for them. If one of your suppliers offers a special discount on a limited number of products, then make sure to get this message across to all bargain hunters. Don't waste the discount on customers who would normally buy at full price no questions asked, unless you are trying to cross-sell them into a new category (see 'share of wallet/cross-sell' below).

Birthday is perhaps the most common of all triggers. Reaching out to customers because their birthday is approaching is a tactic applied across many product and service types, which means you have to be creative in order to distinguish your communication. We often see poor examples of this, for example when a customer receives an email birthday wish from a brand that is not personalized, does not take into account product history and does not include offers for products or discounts. A good use of such an opportunity is motivating customers to use the wishlist function and share it with their peers; you can also suggest relevant products they could add to the list. And of course give them something too – after all, it's their birthday! Acknowledging that they probably have closer friends than you to celebrate their birthday with, see whether you can offer them something they can use in the days around their birthday and not exclusively on the birthday itself. A discount is always nice, but consider giveaways from suppliers, collection samples, special events or similar. If you have physical stores, then ideally this should be something that has the customer come to the store so they can be tempted by other products.

Anniversary is similar to 'birthday'. It could be your customer's wedding anniversary that is triggering this. Data could be submitted by the customers themselves, or you could use AI techniques such as the one described for Interflora above to infer likely dates. It could also be fun to remind the customer that now it is *your common* anniversary – that, for instance, it's one year since they signed up for a club membership, or they've just completed purchase number ten. Use this occasion to delight the customer by acknowledging the history you have together, reminding them that you value this relationship and providing a relevant offer to them.

Plan threshold is used for two things. First, it is a service reminder to tell customers that they are very close to reaching a plan threshold, such as Gold Membership; second, it is used to tell them that this has happened. A new threshold may open up extra benefits, such as earning double points on purchases, the option for customers to choose their own seat on a flight, or even the ability to choose a benefit of their choice.

Share of wallet/cross-sell is often the hardest sell. It's usually easier to sell something to a customer that they've already bought (provided that it's something that gets consumed, of course). However, if you carry a wide assortment, then there can be a lot of extra revenue to be gained by cross-selling new categories to existing customers, thereby increasing customer lifetime value significantly. AI and predictive analytics are scalable ways of finding customers that are eligible to buy something in a new category. Using data from online browsing behaviour, look-a-like models comparing behavioural patterns between customers and product affinities can be quite effective. As soon as you see a propensity for buying into a new category exceeding a certain threshold for a customer, that's the moment you've been looking for. But make sure not to set the threshold too low or you'll come across as being spammy.

Local and personalized newsletter and **local event** can be approached similarly to a normal newsletter. The difference can be sending the newsletter from a store near to where the customer lives or with which they have a special connection. Allow the store manager to influence what is in the newsletter and incorporate content that is specific to this location. What's going on in this particular city or neighbourhood that could increase relevance and strengthen the relationship? Is there a local event that the customer could find interesting? Make sure to add the local store manager in the 'from' address of the newsletter and consider inserting their image or even signature.

Out of stock/back in stock is meant for when a customer has been browsing or asking for a specific item (in a specific size). If this item is out of stock, be sure to make the customer aware of similar or alternative products that could be of interest, or ask them whether they want a reminder once the item is back on the shelves. AI can give you clues as to which customers are likely to be interested in an alternative and help to select which one(s) to offer. As soon as the item does come back in stock, make sure you tell the customer.

Store proximity is a tactic mostly applied within mobile. When a customer is close to a certain store within opening hours, make sure they are alerted of their current personal discounts or any other special benefit that may incite them to visit the store. This can also be used inside department stores for cross-selling across departments, e.g. promoting the food court after a certain amount of time spent shopping.

Service reminder is similar to 'transactional follow-up' but generally happens much later. Some items need a service check after a period of time. A bicycle has to get its brakes and spokes adjusted at some point, parts in a car have to be changed for maintenance and people's eyesight has to be checked regularly by their optician. Make sure to automate this opportunity for reconnecting with your customers.

Retain

In general, you could argue that retaining a retail customer is in part done by trying to develop the customer relation-ship. But when things do start to go south there are still a few arrows left in the quiver.

Points expiring is a subtle way of trying to win back custom-ers. If you've launched a points scheme, then hopefully points will expire at some point. It will most likely be perceived as a service to tell customers about them having points that will expire soon. Tell them how many points are expiring and when. You should also include suggestions as to which items they could use the points for. AI can help you identify who will be most amenable to this type of persuasion and what sort of incentives might convince them.

Net promoter score (**NPS**) is a popular form of customer satisfaction survey. Instead of asking about the customer's satisfaction, you ask customers how likely they are to recommend you to a friend or colleague on a scale from 0 to 10. If they answer between 0 and 6 then obviously you need to address this, learn what went wrong and possibly remedy the damage done. If they answer 9 or 10 – as in, they really want to recommend you – then show them how to do this and possibly provide an incentive to make sure it happens. Offer both parties a benefit if the recommendation is successful. Chapter 5 provides more information about how NPS can be used to obtain valuable insights to optimize your business as a whole. And, as described in Chapter 3, note how Cablecom used AI to learn from this type of feedback and predict satisfaction levels across all customers.

Repermission is a way of letting customers know that you've noticed their engagement has dropped, and then trying to get this back up. You trigger this tactic by looking at the time since the last email was opened, the last purchase, the last login or similar, or by having an AI model recognize more subtle signs of impending disengagement. Instead of just keeping up the steady pace of campaigns, try addressing the fact that engagement is dropping. Have the customer re-opt in or give them the possibility of lowering the communication frequency. This not only shows the customer that you are paying attention but also helps your sender reputation with email service providers. When you lower the frequency for (or even unsubscribe) unengaged customers, your average opening rates go up and this will strengthen your general deliverability, avoiding spam complaints and bad placements in for instance the inboxes of Gmail and Hotmail.

Win-back offer is the last resort. It's been too long since you've seen any monetary action from a customer. They must be spending their money elsewhere. Addressing this directly through communication, and using discounts and relevant products and events as bait, are usually the best ways of getting the customer back. Use AI to help you select the bait that's most likely to work in each case. You could also use this moment to learn more about why the customer doesn't shop with you anymore. Ask them why and show your appreciation for this small favour. Maybe posing this question will make them reconsider. Ironically, doing you a favour can make them like you better.

Subscription

Subscription businesses reuse many of the tactics from retail. Personalized permission capture, personalized newsletters, profile surveys, repermission, win-back offers and such tactics are also completely valid for subscription businesses and thus we haven't repeated the description of those below. Instead you will find details of each new subscription-specific tactic to provide you with inspiration below.

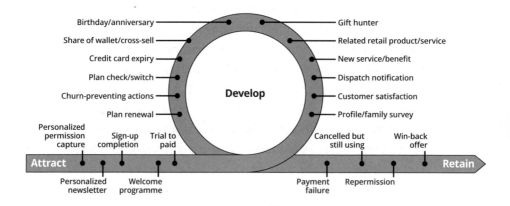

Attract

Sign-up completion is a tactic that resembles the abandoned basket tactic from retail. In this moment you'll find all potential customers who almost completed a purchase but didn't. It could be that you have collected their permission and can communicate directly to them through app push messages, browser notifications, email or similar. Remind them that they almost completed something and you've saved their progress, so they don't have to start from scratch again. AI can help to determine which customers are most likely to complete the sign-up and should be your focus; it can also predict which 'nudge' will best persuade them to do so.

Welcome programme is also a valid tactic in subscription. In contrast to a retail scenario, you'll likely want to spend some time informing the customer of all the options and benefits that are available within the service. Use insights from your data analytics and make sure that you motivate customers to do relevant things that lead to a high customer lifetime value. Encourage them to download the app, set up shortcuts to the service and give advice on how to use the application or app properly to get them off to a good start. Keep track of what they in fact do and remind them to do the rest.

Trial to paid is only valid if you use trial subscriptions in your process of acquiring new subscribers. You can argue that converting trial subscribers into paying customers starts with a good welcome programme; however, as the expiration date of the trial approaches, it makes sense to start addressing all the benefits of being a real paying customer and what exactly this entails. If the customer has been using the trial subscription heavily, then consider pointing this out to them using the engagement data you have available and show how much value and/or joy the customer is likely experiencing by using the service. Also make sure to communicate all the practical information around becoming a real customer. Do you need extra information? Billing information? Based on behaviour during the trial period, AI can give a reliable prediction of how likely each customer is to convert. For customers at risk of not converting, you can consider extending the trial period and relaunch a light version of the welcome programme.

Develop

Dispatch notification is primarily used within businesses that issue publications such as magazines. When a new issue is ready and in the post, it's a good time to inform the subscriber so they can look forward to receiving the publication. Just because something drops into the mailbox these days, it doesn't mean that the subscriber notices it. Make sure to include reasons as to why the subscriber should bother opening the magazine – which articles are included that fit the profile of this particular subscriber? AI can help you identify which content matches their likely preferences.

New service/benefit is the moment you launch a new product or benefit to your subscribers. It could be a new type of add-on subscription, such as nutritional supplements included in a fitness club membership, or a general benefit, such as a special retail discount available for subscribers. This service/benefit should be communicated to customers for whom it's relevant, or to customers identified by predictive models as having a high propensity to take it on. Make sure to not only launch the service/benefit via a dedicated campaign, but also include it in your existing automated communications, such as the welcome programme.

Related retail product/service is used by subscription services that have an attached e-commerce store. It can be hard to justify to existing subscribers that new customers get welcome gifts while loyal subscribers get nothing. So, quite often, it's a good idea to let existing customers shop limited items with an attractive discount. When a product pops up that is relevant to certain subscribers, make sure to tell them and also include this in your normal tactics. As with retail, you can use AI to determine which products are the best fit for each customer and which customers are likely to be tempted by specific levels of discount.

Share of wallet/cross-sell is a bit different from in retail. Instead of selling products, consider other types of subscription a customer could be interested in. Affinity to a certain subscription along with third-party data on addresses from the customer's neighbourhood can very well indicate that certain other subscriptions are relevant. If they are subscribing to a fashion magazine, could they also be interested in subscribing to a kids' magazine? Could they need high-speed internet along with their electricity? Association algorithms and models that predict customers' propensity to take specific additional subscriptions can help to guide the offers you make.

Credit card expiry is probably the one 'must-do' tactic for all subscriptions. It's so easy and can seriously avoid a lot of unnecessary churn. When the expiration date of a credit card approaches, make sure you remind the customer in due time. Chances are that they've already received the new credit card from their bank and, if they are happy using the service, they'll be pretty sure to change the card that is attached to your subscription, provided you remind them. AI techniques can help to identify any latent causes of dissatisfaction that may cause them to hesitate and you can plan to pre-empt these.

Plan check/switch communications should be sent at regular intervals. Even if nothing has happened, reassure the customer they've made the right choice and they are on the right plan, or encourage them to switch to something more appropriate if your data shows you this is better for them. Could they have a lower monthly bill if they switched to a variable rate for their electricity? Would they be better off with a phone subscription that included free international roaming? Or flat-fee voice conversation? Perhaps it will mean a slightly lower recurring revenue for you, but it's better than the customer feeling they've paid more than they had to. That would make them vulnerable to acquisition activities from your competitors. The AI techniques we discussed in Chapter 3, including optimization, can help you to ensure you match the best tariff to each customer across your subscriber base.

Churn-preventing actions can be applied at any point in the customer's relationship with you and will often be brought into play as a result of an AI model detecting likely churn risk. This is a place where the 'next best action' approach (described in Chapter 3) is often applied, to select the optimal action that will secure the best long-term outlook for your relationship with the customer.

Plan renewal is probably what you want your subscribers to do. If you've played your cards right, this will simply involve a service announcement informing the customer that renewal has happened. If there is a churn risk and you're able to anticipate this ahead of time (perhaps with the aid of a predictive model), offer the right benefit or gift to the customers that show a high risk of leaving you for a competitor.

Retain

Payment failure is the moment that a credit card failure is experienced. Most often this is not because the customer wished to cancel their subscription but merely because they cannot remember all the places where their credit card is in use. For instance, when they change banks, their card expires, and suddenly some recurring payments stop working.

Follow up on this with simple instructions on how to supply new information and reinstate their subscription.

Cancelled but still using occurs when subscriptions offer customers the option of using the subscription even after the cancellation. When data shows this is taking place, you have a pretty good candidate for a special 'early win-back offer'. You can ask the customer whether they would like to sign up again – perhaps without a start-up fee.

RELEVANCE TACTICS

Getting the timing right is a good step towards becoming relevant, though it is by no means a universal tactic that can always be applied and that will serve all needs. In this section we'll explore other relevance tactics.

Below is an introduction to a number of tactics you can apply in order to make your customers feel that a communication is suited to them, thus increasing your chances of getting your message across. These tactics can be used across channels, on large and small scales, and be used simultaneously for increased impact. Sorted by the degree to which they support a feeling of customer centricity, they can be placed in the Omnichannel Hexagon's blue pyramid, as shown below.

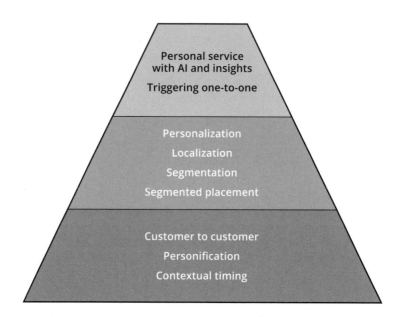

Contextual timing

Contextual timing means that you time your message to coincide with something going on in the world right now. It could be a big event or maybe just tonight's TV schedule. The timing could also be weather dependent. The concept is also known by the term 'real-time marketing'.

Pizza Hut in the UK uses personalization tools on its website to time and localize its coupons according to the local weather forecast. If it promises to be a nice sunny day, Pizza Hut knows from its data that it will usually not be as busy in the restaurant as it might want. Therefore, it provides coupons and communicates about them to customers on days with good weather, so it will be easier to fill up the restaurants.

Personification

Personification (not to be confused with personalization) is about sending the message from another name than the brand itself. The communication seems more human as there is a personal sender at the other end. In TV, brands often use celebrities to talk about the product in an ad or as an extension of good PR work, or more subtly as product placement in an entertainment programme.

But this tactic also works during more personal one-to-one dialogue. Certain brands feature experts – real and fictional alike – who speak on the brand's behalf about relevant topics. On an email level, the 'from' name in the inbox can be a real person and if the customer hits the 'reply' button then it can appear that this person will actually receive the answer. The content is written in a personal style, with only a few branding elements and maybe a scanned signature to finish the email off. So, it appears quite personal, but the content and timing of the message can still be automated.

Customer to customer

Even if you do not necessarily have much data on your customers, thorough market insight on a global level can be extremely effective for getting close to something that feels significant and relevant to a large group of customers. An example of this is when the manufacturer of sanitary pads and tampons Always hit the world with its #likeagirl campaign. By directing people's attention towards how adolescence can create insecurity among female teenagers, Always was able to discreetly stand out as part of the solution.

Often a big campaign through paid media can get these conversations started. Over the past few years we've seen companies starting to use influencers in addition to (or sometimes even a substitution for) traditional media. Influencers are individuals who have large followings on social media and who are worthy and authentic carriers of the message you want out there, whether it's a complex story or simply a new product.

Segmented placement

Even on the channels where it is hard or impossible to target the right message to specific individual customers, there is still an opportunity to do some kind of segmentation in the placement you choose for your message.

If it's outdoors, then you know that there are certain types of people who live in specific cities and neighbourhoods. The same applies to placement in a TV advertising block or insertion of a banner. Certain channels, shows and times of day increase the exposure to the attractive target groups, as opposed to the less attractive.

Segmentation

Segmentation is about deciding who will get a certain message. You divide customers into groups that share certain characteristics. Some of these characteristics are more permanent than others. Gender, for instance, is permanent for the vast majority of people, whereas subscription status can vary over time. If in your case we're talking about segments built on very dynamic data and updated automatically, then please skip to the paragraph on 'triggering' below.

If you don't know very much about your customers, you can segment based purely on demographic characteristics. If you have a mature setup for data analytics, you may have behaviour-based segments correlated to high and low customer lifetime value or to certain personas.

When you have a certain message, you should decide which segments should receive it, so you don't waste the attention of customers or an unnecessarily high portion of the advertising budget on burdening indifferent leads with irrelevant messages. Note that if you are getting attention through paid media then segments are often referred to as 'audiences'.

Localization

Localization rests somewhere between segmentation and personalization. Although it does not involve personalizing based on directly personal data, it is still effective and advisable to localize content to better fit local circumstances. Countries and territories have different cultural heritages that can further vary according to specific underlying ethnicities and religions. So, when you want to launch a global Christmas campaign, keep in mind that not everybody celebrates Christmas and that it isn't winter south of the Equator. Instead of watering your communication down and sending 'Seasonal Greetings' as opposed to 'Merry Christmas', you should consider allowing markets to make true localization by personalizing the message based on the data and knowledge you have of a specific region or country. Consider the religion, climate zone, origin of the (human) models in use, etc. to make the best match. The result should be that people who most likely will be celebrating a white Christmas will get a greeting that matches this – whereas others who are not likely to be celebrating Christmas (but may very well have a few days off) receive the 'Seasonal Greetings'.

More practical things to consider within the localization tactic include which products are actually available for which markets. Additionally, if you put exact promotions and prices in your communication, you have to consider the matter of different currencies.

The global toy company LEGO has used this method when localizing the message of a certain campaign to French and German audiences. For the German audience, the company took a very constructional approach, emphasizing the stuff a father could build together with his children as he had done with his father. But, for the French audience, the company couldn't rely on childhood experiences, since many people had played with the competing brand Playmobil, so it spoke to the mother of the family with a more playful and feminine message.

Personalization

Very broadly, personalization is often taken to mean achieving relevance. We reserve it for when you are communicating directly with a customer and you have to decide *what* to communicate or show – in other words, the specific content of the communication.

It could be that you are personalizing which products to show on an individual level. That's the easy part because the content is already there in your product catalogue, although you have to figure out which products to show to whom, which can be more tricky. If you are personalizing a more substantial or creative piece of content, then you have to decide how many versions are necessary and incorporate the resources needed to do this. If you are skilled in data analytics, you can find input for the answers there (see Chapter 3).

If you are reaching out to all members of a fitness club that have a high risk of cancelling their subscription (a high-risk segment calculated through AI), then it makes sense to vary this message depending on which subsegment a customer belongs to. In order to encourage them to reactivate, senior citizens may need a different message, line of argumentation and tone of voice than would a young man working out to get lean and buff.

Segments calculated from profile data or AI, such as personas, are used to determine how to personalize large pieces of content. When it comes down to product-level personalization, AI should be used to drive automated product recommendations.

Triggering, or one-to-one

Timing, timing, timing – if we had to choose between personalization and timing, the choice would be timing. A relevant message, with the right timing, to the right recipient, will generate a significantly greater effect than nearly any other marketing. One-off actions initiated by specific conditions in the data are known as triggered actions – for example, trigger emails, trigger messages or trigger flows (trigger flows apply if you have multiple interrelated communications going out to a customer that evolve around the same place in the customer lifecycle). Note that triggering needn't be based on manually created conditions; AI models monitoring each customer's data can recognize when it is timely to deliver a message and when to catch the recipient at their most receptive moment. In the section above we already covered a multitude of examples for how you can trigger relevant communication at the right time in the customer lifecycle.

Personal service with AI insights

The relevance tactics mentioned above are mostly related to communication that you can choose to send out to customers. Hopefully, customers will also be seeking you out and you will meet them on your inbound channels. Apart from your website (where the tactics above do also indeed apply) your employees will be meeting customers in the physical store, the customer service centre – whether it be through channels such as chat, on the phone or in a physical meeting. Here, it is of key importance that your employees are informed with the same insights that you utilize in your general outbound communication so that they will have the opportunity to communicate with an equal degree of relevance. If you are able to combine the digital insights with good old-fashioned service and a smile, then your customers are in for a truly memorable customer experience. (Read more about the application of this tactic within retail further below.)

To achieve personal service with AI insights the principle of the next best action (NBA), which we discussed in Chapter 3, can be extremely useful. The NBA is a calculation or determination of which action you should take next to have the most positive effect on the customer's relationship with you. A non-revenue-generating action – or even one with costs, such as a voucher by way of apology for a poor service the customer has had but may not have complained about – might be better than a sales offer because it reduces retention risk and in the long term leads to higher customer lifetime value. The NBA is especially useful for personal interactions in customer service and in-store personal meetings.

How personalization and triggering work together

If you have a large permission base and a lot of data and insights, you can use personalization and triggering together for increased effect.

Say, for instance, that you've launched a welcome flow for new fitness club members. The timing is fairly easy to get right – immediately after signing up, the customer should receive the first message, which could be about how membership works and how to get the most out of it. You'll most likely make a one-size-fits-all welcome flow covering topics such as practical information around getting access to the club and booking classes, the importance of having a training programme, the option of booking personal trainers, the importance of setting a goal for training, etc. Customers will most likely respond fairly well to this, but the response will differ from segment to segment. So, if the general performance is indexed as 100 and you see 'Segment B' (which could be senior citizens) showing only a performance index of 80, then you may need to enhance the flow for this particular segment. Ask yourself how you could vary the messages, the images and the tone of voice to improve the flow for this segment.

	SEGMENT A	SEGMENT B
Generic welcome flow	Performance index: 100	Performance index: 80

	SEGMENT A	SEGMENT B
Generic welcome flow	Performance index: 100	-
Personalized welcome flow for Segment B	-	Performance index: 100

Which tactics to choose

If you are wondering which tactics are best, the answer, unfortunately, is not very straightforward. If you have problems with customer acquisition (bringing in and getting to know customers), it would be natural to go broadly into mass communication using some of the tactics mentioned above. If you already have a lot of customers but face challenges in retaining them or selling more to them, then it makes sense to start the whole journey by collecting permissions and data, finding insights, and then personalizing and timing as many of your communications as possible.

Almost regardless of how much data you get on every single customer, they will over time be exposed to a variety of one-to-one, personalized, segmented and mass communication. The customer will in the course of a month receive personalized emails, push messages on the app, and segmented or general newsletters, but will also see your brand in TV ads, outdoor advertising and less targeted marketing.

The degree of personalization will naturally vary because not all communication channels are equally interconnected and integrated. The trick is to find the point where it is no longer profitable to personalize further – the 'inflexion point'. However, the inflexion point will be in constant motion as you gain volume in your customer base, customer data and insights and as the evolution of media makes it increasingly easier to personalize messages across channels.

Is it profitable to do one-to-one?

The answer is a clear yes, and even to a degree you would not think possible. However, it requires that you have plenty of permissions and data on your customers and your prospects, and that you use this effectively.

The underlying business models behind one-to-one communication and automation are to a great extent incremental, and over time they will create more and more value for the same effort. For instance, a welcome programme runs automatically once it is up and running, creating sustained value day after day. So, to maximize value creation, it's suddenly interesting how fast you can deploy multiple automated communication flows.

CLASSIC OMNICHANNEL COMMERCE FEATURES

Apart from the previously mentioned relevance tactics, there are some classic service features that omnichannel companies within physical retail should seriously consider. Many shoppers consider these to be a given, in which case customer expectations will not be met if most of these are not implemented.

Returning items to store

Few things are as frustrating for a customer as not being able to return an item purchased online to a physical store of the same brand. You are disappointing customers if they are met with messages such as: "Sorry, we don't accept returns from the e-commerce store. That's a different business unit." Incentive structures and some logistics may need to be adjusted to make this work, but it is considered 'table stakes' (a minimum requirement) to allow this.

Click & collect (BOPIS)

Sometimes referred to as BOPIS (buy online and pick up in-store), click & collect is a feature that allows customers to place orders online but pick them up in a store nearby. We saw it in action in the opening narrative of this book, where Debbie picked up an order at Nordstrom. If properly implemented, BOPIS significantly improves online conversion rates and allows for further up-sales in-store.[33] However, make sure stores are able to cope with receiving customers who have ordered online; you can even consider dedicating an area or staff to handle these customers and orders and you should monitor inventory to ensure you have the item in stock.

Endless aisles

Physical retail naturally has a limited assortment in stock. Not all products can be available in all variants and sizes. Smart omnichannel retailers offer the option to purchase online from the store. If a specific variant is not available, then the sales associate still has the option of closing the order by having the item shipped from the online inventory and directly to the customer. Sometimes this is implemented as an in-store kiosk where customers can self-serve.

Split order

Three for the price of two is a good offer. Ideally such promotions should be available for the customer even if they only get two items in-store and order the remaining item to be shipped directly to their home address.

Reserve and collect

This is a variant of click and collect where the payment is postponed until the customer actually picks up the goods. This can further boost conversion rates but takes more effort to implement because it often conflicts with traditional incentive structures (the conversion is moved from online to offline) and because it puts demand on the retailer to put the item aside. This poses high demands for precise inventory management and training of in-store sales associates.

Shipping from store

Though not strictly an omnichannel feature, it's also worth mentioning the option of shipping an item from a store. If a customer has ordered online then a local store could carry out that fulfilment. If you are really good at inventory management, a store where this item is not selling well could ship the item. The ability to ship from store can also avoid many situations of customers experiencing an item to be 'sold out' in the webshop.

Using customer data in-store

Apart from the standard omnichannel commerce tactics mentioned above, customer recognition and access to a comprehensive digital customer profile can make all the difference between success or failure when customers haven't yet made up their mind about a specific purchase. The behaviour of trying on products in the store before buying them online is referred to as 'showrooming' whereas the act of browsing websites before visiting the store is referred to as 'webrooming'.

In the early days of omnichannel, retailers were scared that people would come to their store and spend a lot of the sales associates' time to talk about products and try on different styles just to go home and buy the products from a competing and more discount-focused website. But since there is really no way of preventing customers from doing this, retailers might as well try and get the best of the fact that they have personal contact with the customers.

Data and insights from previous interactions on both digital and physical channels coupled with the immediate response, observations and intimacy that only personal service can give can provide a unique foundation for creating a good customer experience no matter in which order the customer chooses to use the channels. If communication and service are seamless and if it is made easy for the customer to continue the same purchase journey even if they change channels, then chances are that you will win the trust of the customer in the end.

However, there is no easy solution, and this scenario does not come about without some serious integration work. On the other hand, the benefits are substantial in an omnichannel context. And remember, no kind of data insight can make up for a demotivated sales associate who doesn't meet customers with a smile.

Many large brands have tried integrating technology into their stores. Only a few, however, have succeeded in using it to become more personal with the customer. There are a few great examples where it has become more than a gimmick.

One example is IKEA, which makes it possible for customers to take the configuration of a new kitchen quite far before they even consider talking to a sales associate in-store. In the comfort of their home, they can visualize their future kitchen on IKEA's website and make a lot of choices and decisions, as well as get an indication of the price. When they decide to visit the store, the sales associate will ask whether they've already started online. The sales associate will then help the customer find the exact configuration that they've prepared and use their subject matter expertise to help finalize the offer. This saves a lot of time for everybody and ultimately leads to more kitchens being sold.

Another example is the international fashion chain Suitsupply. The first time the customer visits the store, the staff offer to take the customer's measurements, and this data is stored and used whenever the customers wishes. If the customer is online and wants to order a few extra shirts, he can be confident they will fit his body shape perfectly; alternatively, if he's in-store and wants to decide on the style of his new tuxedo, his measurements will be available there too. Suitsupply makes it easy to buy tailor-made clothes by saving and using data across all channels.[34]

GET CLOSE, BUT DON'T GET CREEPY

We are often asked whether or not customers are getting freaked out by all this use of data. When things get creepy, it's often because, although customers are aware that companies are collecting certain types of data, they may not realize the full extent of what this data enables companies to do. For most people it's no surprise that companies are giving personalized product recommendations on their website based on previous purchases. Other types of data collection are subtler and more discreet, and, even when all the consents are in order, they can still be considered creepy. Take the example given in Chapter 2: the fact that Amazon owns IMDB and data is shared between the two.

To avoid freaking customers out with how you use data, you should:
- Consider the age group of the recipient – the older a customer is, the higher the risk of them seeing personalization as creepy (that said, this is a generalization, and there are many exceptions on a personal level).
- Consider how directly you address what triggered your message – if you are basing communications on data that the recipient may be unaware they have given up, then water down the reasoning in the message a bit to make it seem more coincidental that this customer is being exposed to this message right now.
- Consider the communication channel and how normal it is for customers to be addressed personally there.

For instance, very obvious personalization in display banners or on Facebook may be considered creepy.

Combining business rules and AI

Algorithms and AI may be tremendously helpful in scaling personalized communications and messages. However, don't put all your faith in AI to come up with the perfect suggestion. You need humans to evaluate the actual output and apply suitable business rules that work together with the AI.

If AI is not combined with human interaction and business rules, events can take unexpected directions. Human supervision is highly recommended. Take, for instance, the company My Handy Design, which relied on AI to find images from the internet and automatically create customized iPhone covers using these images for sale on Amazon. This ended up with some really hilarious examples of iPhone covers showing adult diapers and even more inappropriate images from the darkest corners of the internet.[35]

A less hilarious but perhaps more widely applicable example is from a sporting goods retailer that applied AI to pick the products most likely to be sold to specific customers. The algorithm did a fine job in selecting these products, but all the products were black, which, even though they may have been technically correct, made for some extremely boring visual emails that failed to inspire anyone.

There will always be exceptions to which recommendations you may want to give. For instance, there's no reason for a grocery store to recommend that people buy milk – they figure that out by themselves. Or perhaps you are carrying some products that need discretion, such as pregnancy tests, sex toys or similar.

THE CHANNELS

It is a thankless job to describe and categorize all the channels on which you can communicate with and serve your customers. We are sure that when we read this section again six years from now, at least one new social medium that everyone thinks we have to be on will have popped up. More traditional media will have gone further along the route towards digitization, perhaps capable of recognizing consumers in completely new contexts. There are already myriad media and channels that companies have to deal with, in principle. In the following text we confine ourselves to the channels listed in the table below.

CHANNEL	DESCRIPTION
TV	Primarily TV commercials (but see 'PR and influencer marketing' below).
Radio	Primarily radio spots (but see 'PR and influencer marketing' below).
Print	Traditionally, household distributed advertisements and insertions in printed matter such as newspapers and magazines (but see 'PR and influencer marketing' below).
Outdoor	Placement of advertisements on bus stops, billboards, facades, posters and the like.
In-store	Exposure in the company's own store network (both own stores and stores-in-stores). Includes in-store screens, customer radio, signage, customer queries by staff, etc.
Packaging	Wrapping of the product and stickers, bottle collars, etc.
Events	Time-limited happenings at particular locations, where the brand is the sender or facilitator.

Call centre	Inbound and outbound call centre activities – i.e. manual handling of telephone calls that either originate in or are received in the company.
Display advertising	Banner advertising that appears in locations other than the company's own website. Placement, real-time bidding, retargeting, etc. can be purchased, including advertising on social media sites such as Facebook, LinkedIn and YouTube.
Search marketing	Advertising on search engines such as Google, Yahoo and Bing.
Website	The company's own websites – both mobile and desktop – can be both sales and marketing channels. These contain both products and rich content for use in content marketing and search engine optimization. Company blogs are also in this category.
App	The company's app, e.g. to be installed via Apple's App Store or Google Play. Apps can contain tools for the user and be used as a channel for push communications, if consent has been given. Has the advantage that you can ask for permission to access data from other installed apps, such as the calendar, image library and the camera to gain extra knowledge on the customer.
Text messaging/ SMS	Text messages sent from the company, but also incoming texts, which can collect data and trigger communication the other way.
Email	Systematized email, such as newsletters and trigger email, as well as manual email communication between the company and customers.
Direct mail	Primarily covers service letters and direct mail from the company.

Social media	Includes e.g. Facebook, Twitter, LinkedIn, YouTube and Instagram. Arguably the most dynamic category. Once upon a time there was just Myspace, but since then we've seen Google+, Pinterest, Snapchat etc. Extends over paid, owned and earned media; can be an incubator for viral marketing, especially if it is helped by a large media budget and the right influencers are approached or paid to carry the message.
PR and influencer marketing	PR is more a discipline than it is a channel. Covers the work of getting the company's story and products mentioned and/or talked about on others' media, whether this is centrally controlled media (such as TV), newspapers or magazines, or the media channels of influencers on social media. Digital PR has the advantage that it often involves links back to the company's website, which has a positive influence on the company's Google ranking.
Devices	Devices are a relatively new category. This category covers the possibility of being able to interact with customers via the digitized products the customer buys – e.g. communication to and from a Tesla car, or notifications from an Apple Watch or a Fitbit. Still a young category, but one that it will be exciting to follow.
Chatbot	This is also a relatively new category. Chatbots are automated bots used for customer service questions and similar. They are powered by more or less simplistic algorithms and AI using natural language processing and a large knowledge base that enables them to give the right answers to the most common questions. As AI and algorithms mature, we imagine a future where customers will prefer chatting to a bot as opposed to a newly hired customer service rep.

Does a company have to be on every channel for it to be true omnichannel?

It would never make sense to be present on all channels, since it would never be profitable. Narrow your usage to the channels that you have the resources to tie into a total customer experience rather than spreading yourself too thin just for the sake of having a presence. This varies across markets and geographical regions. For instance, in China it makes sense to be on WeChat. In Europe, that's not a concern.

How are the channels distinguished?

It can be difficult to assess what role each channel should play in the customer journey. As an aid to these reflections, we will address some issues that will help to distinguish the channels and establish their priority, in relation to both where the media are today and where they are going.

Paid, owned and earned media

In recent years, the notion of paid, owned and earned media has gained ground. Every time you need to draw attention to your brand and your product, you have in principle a choice of how much to use paid, owned and earned media. We briefly touched upon this classification in Chapter 1. Below we'll go into a bit more detail.

Paid media are, not surprisingly, those where a company must pay to expose a given target group to a message. Traditional TV, newspaper and outdoor advertising fall into this category, naturally. Usually some kind of segmentation is offered – for example, before which TV shows or in which trade journal an ad will be shown. Careful selection of outdoor locations can also be a basis of segmentation.

Paid media also includes many of the digital advertising options. Although we can make it very intelligent and personalized with retargeting (re-exposing website visitors through display ads) and twin audiences (i.e. audiences that display web behaviour comparable to an initial group's behaviour), all online banner advertising is still paid media. Similarly, Google AdWords, in particular, has become a big expense for many advertisers, and there is nothing to suggest that this is about to change.

Earned media covers the brand's earned reputation. This category includes mentions in the press, on social media, on blogs and (some will say) in organic search traffic from Google (i.e. the part that is not AdWords). Many would argue that the exposure that can be gained on Facebook, Twitter and Instagram constitutes earned media. Every time someone decides that your content is worth sharing, that is earned reputation.

Unfortunately, the fact is that even if you have already spent quite a lot of money getting your customers to 'like' your page on Facebook or follow you on Twitter, you will only reach a few with your posts. Analysis shows that on Facebook it is typically fewer than 5% of your followers[36] who will see a given post, unless you pay to expose more of your followers to the message. However, you have then, in our opinion, crossed over into the category of paid media.

Owned media are the channels you yourself control and can use without having to pay other businesses. They include all the existing touchpoints that you have with customers and prospects. It could be your storefront, your store layout, your in-store TV or your website: all inbound or 'pull' media (i.e. those that you depend on customers seeking out before you can reach them with a message). In addition, there is your own outbound or 'push' media. These most often consist of your email and customer base, and, if you are more advanced, your mobile permissions as well, whether text messages or messages you push directly to an app that you know the customer has installed. Your own call centre can also be both an inbound and an outbound owned medium. Direct mail is another owned medium; however, the cost per direct mail is so relatively large that it is debatable whether or not it is actually paid media.

Connected versus unconnected

Whether a channel is connected, i.e. linked with data to your marketing ecosystem, or not makes all the difference in enabling true bidirectional communication. An unconnected channel can provide fine exposure and encourage interaction via a different channel. It could be 2D bar codes on your packaging, or invitations to send a text message with a specific short code to a particular number or to enter a specific URL in a browser. With few exceptions, the traditional media are most often not connected; this applies to TV, radio, print and outdoor ads.

It goes without saying that digital channels are more connected than analogue channels. However, there is a clear dividing line between the anonymized cookie network used by media agencies and the whole personal marketing ecosystem that your own digital media comprise. As an advertiser, you can indeed target banner ads to specific groups of individuals but due to legal issues their true identity is never a part of the media agencies' cookie systems. So getting data back into your own ecosystem from potential interactions in paid media is generally not possible. There is also a limit to how much information you may be allowed to integrate *from* the ecosystems of media such as Facebook. They are, after all, most interested in keeping the dialogue with the customer on their channel, preferably (from their point of view) with some form of paid advertising involved. Although many channels are still not connected, there is an evolution going on within this field, with more and more channels being digitized.

Possibility of targeting messages

The digital channels usually have greater potential for targeting messages to either segments or individuals than the analogue channels do. Direct mail is perhaps an exception, since the starting point for the production of letters is most often a database where each letter is subjected to hefty mail-merging of various pieces of personal information and messages. Digital channels such as websites, email, text messages and apps are at the summit of message-targeting potential, but personally operated media (such as the call centre, customer service, social media and in-store service) also have the potential for completely personal and targeted efforts. The accuracy with which you can target messages again depends on how connected a channel is.

Push and pull

There is a great difference between whether a channel allows for actively pushing messages to customers or not. The whole difference lies in whether you have to cross your fingers and hope that your customer happens to drop by, or can actively do something to get their attention.

There are different degrees of push. A notification buzzing on a phone gets the greatest attention. A non-boosted post on your company's Facebook page is also a push, but, as we have previously described, you will be dependent on Facebook finding it relevant enough to show it to your followers.

At the extreme pull end of the spectrum is your website. If you have good content on your website, where you write about things people are actually interested in, there is a chance that you will get a good amount of organic non-paid search traffic from Google. Content – both text and images – that is so good and illustrative that people want to share, mention and link to it will then give another boost to your site's Google's ranking. Altogether, this effort could also have a positive impact on how much you need to pay for a click when you need to advertise on AdWords. This is also regarded as a pull medium, since the limit on how much traffic you can create is determined by customer search volume. However, AdWords is a bit pushier than your website, because you can freely choose which search words you will advertise on.

Automation

If you want to deliver on the tactic of one-to-one personalization and timing and not drown in manual work, you should consider automation. You won't get far if you have to manually send individual text messages to a customer base of 1,000,000.

Email, text messages, app notifications and website content personalization provide full potential for automating the communication in all imaginable ways. There are several major players in this market that want to be the one to give you the tools to orchestrate cross-channel communication. You should take this seriously and get started sooner rather than later.

Automation is also possible for search engine marketing (AdWords), display banners and social media. TV, print and radio are at present more difficult to automate, but, again, they are gradually opening up new ways to buy media exposure. Read more about putting together your marketing technology stack in the section of this name below.

How to manage it all?

As the above sections clearly indicate, there is a lot to consider when you want to manage communications with a large customer base that continually changes channels while maximizing relevance for each individual.

Make centralized data available for the marketing and CRM teams

As discussed in Chapter 2, one of the central components you need to establish in order to succeed with omnichannel is making centralized data available to the marketing and CRM (customer relationship management) teams. There are many ways to accomplish this, but the deployment of customer data platforms and data management platforms is an important aspect. Some of the so-called (see below) marketing hubs also carry this functionality. The deployment of these types of system makes it possible for marketing and CRM to act more freely when it comes to using and experimenting with data. They will be able to put together dynamic target groups and audiences for specific purposes, automation flows, campaigns and detailed segmentation. But the data part is only one half of the equation.

Messages should also be managed centrally

It is important to store data centrally, but data doesn't achieve anything alone. No difference is made until data is combined with your key messages and the result is presented to the right audience. We have to make a distinction here between messages and content. 'Messages' are the pieces of creative content (a combination of text, images and/or video) that are supposed to pique the interest of the audience and lead them to do something they might not have done otherwise, whether that is buying a product, reading more about something or performing a specific action. By 'content' we mean rich articles or pieces of information, most often stored in a content management system (CMS).

Unfortunately, messages are more often than not created and kept in the systems managing each communication channel. The words of a text message are created in a text-messaging system, the text and layout of an email are created in an email system, the personalized content on a website is created in the CMS, etc. This makes creation, coordination, distribution and reporting extremely cumbersome. If you choose to create and store these messages centrally and on a meta level – in other words, before they reach a channel – then you'll be heading towards a much better way of using data and insights in omnichannel marketing. In this way, messages will be flexible and adaptable to multiple communication channels and they will carry different versions or propositions for personalization. Only a very few tools offer this possibility, but look out for it when you are piecing together your marketing technology (martech) stack.

WHAT YOU'VE ALWAYS BEEN DOING AND WHAT YOU'VE NEVER BEEN DOING

The heading for this paragraph describes the challenge in transitioning into the new marketing paradigm. Even if you manage to get all the new things right – think, build and deploy large programs of trigger-based and relevant communications and supply personnel with the right tools and insights to be as relevant as possible – there will always be customers (or potential customers) for whom you hold little or no data. For these customers it is almost impossible to be relevant. Does that mean you should stop doing mass marketing? The bad news of omnichannel marketing is that it does not relieve you from doing what you've always been doing – at least, it won't do so in the foreseeable future. Instead, it gives you more work in a domain where you're probably not as comfortable and skilled. So, if you're already up to your neck in work, it's practically impossible to become a success. Marketing will need more resources for sure, and so will IT.

PIECING TOGETHER YOUR MARKETING TECHNOLOGY STACK

Yes, you'll be needing new tools. In this section we'll focus on demystifying some of the TLAs (two- or three-letter acronyms) that you are most likely to encounter when setting up your martech stack. We've aimed to focus on the main categories that are relevant for omnichannel marketing. It will by no means be an exhaustive list as the categories overlap to a great extent and many systems contain elements from multiple categories simultaneously. Note that we already covered customer data platforms and data management platforms in Chapter 2.

Customer relationship management systems

Customer relationship management (CRM) systems are an old category of systems primarily invented for B2B (business-to-business) contexts where salespeople would extensively take note of their customers and what they talked to them about. More specifically, CRM systems contain information about contacts, leads, opportunities, activities and tasks. They are mostly used for supporting person-to-person contact between salespeople and customers, but some have evolved to include basic capabilities within email marketing.

Marketing automation platforms

Marketing automation platforms (MAPs) are designed for automating as much outbound communications going out to end customers as possible. These platforms often have built-in email marketing capabilities for use in both campaign-based and automated communications. This category has become almost synonymous with B2B lead generation and lead nurturing. Note that, in the Nordic countries, MAPs are equally often seen as B2C offerings that cover most of the characteristics of MMHs (see below).

Multichannel marketing hubs

The multichannel marketing hub (MMH) is the research company Gartner's category for platforms encompassing segmenting, communicating and reporting on an end-customer level (in regard to both campaigns and automation). MMHs carry the opportunity to do this on not just one channel but, as the name suggests, on multiple channels. The category is not very commonly used outside the Gartner ecosystem.

Demand-side platforms

A demand-side platform (DSP) is a tool that rests on top of a data management platform and allows companies (those that 'demand' advertising) to control their own media buying, advertising and data exchanges. A DSP combines multiple methods of buying ads, such as programmatic buying, real-time bidding and retargeting.

Content management systems

A content management system (CMS) is basically a system for building and maintaining websites and the content therein. Many CMS providers see the core CMS offering as commoditized and have moved into the categories that are more closely related to customer experience. However, their core strengths are still around the website and its management.

Social media management

Social media management (SMM) tools offer the possibility of centrally managing multiple social media networks and accounts. Their functionality includes distributing content, listening for specific keywords, managing paid social (social media ads) and reporting on posts and campaigns.

Influencer relationship management systems

As the reach of traditional media (such as TV and print advertising) declines, influencer relationship management (IRM) systems have seen a boost in popularity. Influencers are private people with large groups of followers across social media sites, such as Instagram, Facebook, YouTube and Twitter. An IRM system can help companies to discover and choose relevant influencers to co-market their products, cause or offering; it can also help companies to reach out to influencers, create campaigns and report on them. IRM systems are especially used within the fashion- and life-style-oriented sectors.

Digital asset management

Digital asset management (DAM) systems are used for controlling and managing marketing assets centrally to support the use of these assets across the various marketing functions. This type of platform is optimized to store and serve large volumes of rich content, and it supports the workflows needed to put these central assets in place.

Marketing resource management

Marketing resource management (MRM) systems are used for controlling and managing marketing processes between employees, vendors, agencies and assets as effectively as possible.

What is a marketing cloud, or experience cloud?

A marketing or experience cloud is a wide set of tools and offerings beneath the same brand umbrella. Most of these clouds or suites have been put together through the acquisition of previous best-of-breed vendors from the underlying categories. While the promise is that these underlying systems are all well integrated and act as one platform, this is quite often not the case. And, with the history of the underlying systems all being best-of-breed vendors, it's often just as easy to cherry pick well-functioning parts of suites and make them work in ecosystems across different clouds.

MATURITY IN COMMUNICATION & SERVICE

So, what represents maturity in the use of data and insight in your communication and service?

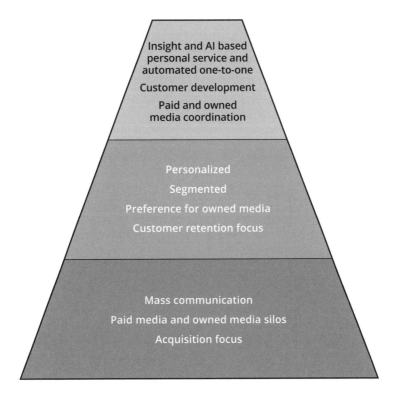

Insight and AI based personal service and automated one-to-one

Customer development

Paid and owned media coordination

Personalized

Segmented

Preference for owned media

Customer retention focus

Mass communication

Paid media and owned media silos

Acquisition focus

Highest maturity level

The mature companies work at learning (from both a human and an AI perspective) as much as possible about customers and prospects. This impacts the way in which they communicate with and service customers on all channels. They provide data-informed, personal service, both in-store and via call centres. In parallel, they constantly work to launch ever more automated personal communication based on data and insights. Their focus is on developing all customer relationships from a one-to-one perspective, where the customer's place in the lifecycle determines what the next move is. There is full synergy between the use of paid and owned media.

Middle maturity level

Companies with average maturity still focus mostly on a company-centric campaign plan and how to apply this most effectively in owned media and paid media. For this purpose, they use data and insights to segment and personalize communications in their campaigns.

However, there is also a long-term goal of gradually building up data and permissions so as to be able to automate communications based on the customer lifecycle. Work is done in both owned and paid media, but they are treated as two separate things, and optimal synergy between them is not yet achieved.

Lowest maturity level

This maturity level designates companies that apply data and insight in their communication poorly. They mainly use paid media via mass communication to create demand and stimulate sales and customer access.

Remember that you can take our test based on the Omnichannel Hexagon and find your company's omnichannel maturity level at:

OMNICHANNELFORBUSINESS.ORG

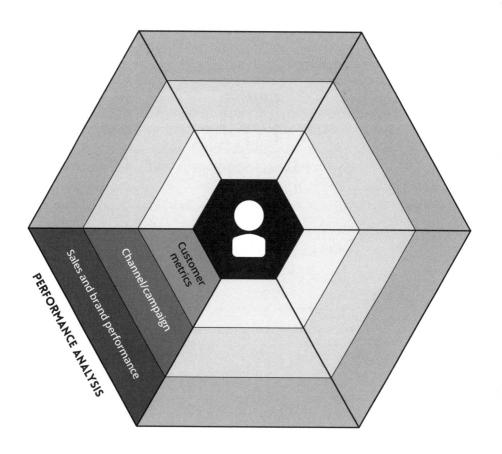

Customer
metrics

Channel/campaign

Sales and brand performance

PERFORMANCE ANALYSIS

5

PERFORMANCE ANALYSIS

If you are undertaking omnichannel marketing and want to follow up on whether it works, then you may have to start monitoring different metrics from the ones you are used to. Customer focus is also important in the way you do performance analysis.

Rasmus is a digital sales manager within Telenor, a Nordic telecommunications company. Over the past few years Telenor has pursued an aggressive omnichannel strategy and everybody has become obsessed with looking at the business in an omnichannel perspective as opposed to a channel perspective.

Rasmus wonders whether conversion rates could be even higher if customer payments were postponed until people were in the store. He got the idea by looking at numbers from the website. When Telenor first gave customers the opportunity to pick up ordered items in the store (click and collect), it had no idea that so many people would take advantage of this feature. If that's the preference, how about giving customers the option to also postpone the payment until they are in the store?

Before the transformation, Rasmus would never have come up with an idea such as this, because moving the payment to the store also means moving the sale to the store. If he were too obsessed with his numbers this idea would actually be counterproductive – for him at least – but there's a good chance it would be a brilliant idea for Telenor.

He discusses the idea with his manager. They agree to try it out and that Rasmus can put together a team to implement it. If it turns out to be a good idea, Telenor will close more sales and they'll fix the attribution and reward issue later.

WHY SHOULD WE REGARD PERFORMANCE ANALYSIS AS A DISTINCT DISCIPLINE?

The Telenor example shows that the customer focus within performance analysis means the company now makes decisions in a different way. Before the omnichannel transformation, Rasmus would have chosen solely to optimize his own slice of the pie even if that would have been a bad decision from his employer's point of view. But now he has the knowledge and the metrics to prove he's making the right decision for Telenor. And, quite importantly, he is confident that his manager will adjust Rasmus's personal incentive programme to incorporate the revenue generated from the experiment.

The knowledge gained from its work with data analytics has shown Telenor that there can be more pie for everybody if different departments stop focusing solely on goals and metrics that correspond to their specific departments and instead focus on customer metrics. Modern customers don't restrict themselves to interacting through only one channel – they choose exactly the channels that are convenient. So, in a way, customers are transcending channels – and so should the metrics. How else will you know you're succeeding with omnichannel if you do not measure your success on customer metrics?

The next question is how mature your culture is in terms of ensuring updated numbers and targets are available. In most organizations the old 'truths' and gut feelings end up framing the decisions that are made. Therefore, there is great value in being among those who know, rather than those who simply believe and feel. As the famous statistician W. Edwards Deming is commonly thought to have said: "Without data, you're just a man with an opinion."

Correct, updated figures are important in a constantly changing world

The digitalization of everyday life has enhanced communication and thus the speed at which we develop ourselves, businesses and our world. Now, consumers change habits more often and more quickly than in the past. Suddenly, a competitor introduces a similar product to your cash cow, Amazon decides to open showrooms and initiate overnight delivery in your region, or your competition launches a new digital service that pulls the rug out from under your feet.

You are living in a world that is constantly changing at an unprecedented pace. You may well wonder whether your decision-makers have the insights needed to evaluate the impact of potential marketing efforts. Without updated and documentable knowledge, worse decisions will be made.

Once the decisions have been made and the projects initiated, it is important to be able to follow up and assess the impact of the efforts. Is it going as well as you expected? What are the fresh figures on your efforts?

You have to work with performance analysis in such a way that the discipline will be instrumental in your way of assessing and optimizing your business performance. This does not just apply to senior decision-makers but to employees in all functions on all levels. Imagine if you could give all these employees the ability to make informed decisions on the basis of relevant, updated metrics.

Performance analysis for the employee

For individual employees, performance analysis is an important aspect of documenting the effect of a little extra effort. It provides a realistic picture of how well employees are performing. It also allows them to see whether they are making good decisions and thus enables them to perform better in the long run.

Performance analysis for the company

As a company, you have to measure efficiently in order to better navigate within the available budgets. You have to use performance analysis to make active decisions about efforts to be initiated and how they perform. In addition, you should use performance analysis when annual or quarterly budgets are created, with the funds to be distributed among the various cost centres within your organization.

This chapter focuses on conducting performance analysis as a distinct and important discipline within omnichannel marketing. First, we will review what you should measure, then we will focus on more general topics within performance analysis. After that, we will go over some of the dangers that can come from being overly numbers-focused in your way of doing business. Finally, we will sum up the characteristics of high maturity in performance analysis in an omnichannel perspective.

WHAT SHOULD YOU MEASURE?

It will be appropriate to monitor various metrics, depending on your industry and sector. This chapter will focus on metrics (key performance indicators, or KPIs) related to sales, branding and customer-related issues, i.e. not metrics for supply chains, production efficiency, related costs, etc.

By focusing on the discipline Performance Analysis in the Omnichannel Hexagon, we see that it is divided into three maturity levels. In the following sections, we will move progressively deeper into the centre of the model within the discipline.

Maturity level 1 – sales and brand performance
Sales numbers

It is a legal obligation to measure a company's turnover and financial results. Therefore, you will find this KPI in the outermost maturity ring of the Omnichannel Hexagon. Turnover is often measured more frequently than once a year. On the store level, the receipts are often tallied daily to assess whether it was a good or a bad day. On the corporate level, this is often done quarterly and monthly. Comparisons are made with the planned budget for the financial year to date, to see whether the business is on track or not.

Sales are often tallied per sales channel, to provide a little more insight and to make it possible to use the figure as a control parameter. How large is the turnover on the regional and store levels? What do you spend for B2B (business-to-business) versus B2C (business-to-consumer), and what do you earn on the bottom line? Are things going as planned?

Market share

In industries and product categories where the market is saturated and without significant growth, results are often expressed in market share. Examples of these industries are gasoline suppliers and utility companies.

Brand awareness

Brand awareness or familiarity is a frequently used measure of how widely your brand is known. You can work at quantifying brand awareness through consumer surveys, and familiarity is most often assessed as a percentage of respondents who show either unaided awareness (e.g. "What soft drink brands you can name?") or aided awareness (e.g. "Do you know the Pepsi brand?").

Especially with respect to introducing a new product, brand awareness is important in assessing the extent to which advertising campaigns are effective in getting the brand into top-of-mind awareness among consumers. Very well-established brands also work intensely at maintaining brand awareness. This is an essential parameter for fast-moving consumer goods, because these products do not differ much in terms of their objective product criteria. For example, Coca Cola and Pepsi taste more or less the same, so the choice of one or the other can be determined by which brand we have been most exposed to and what we associate with each one.

Brand perception

This brings us to how your brand is perceived. It is of course relevant what consumers think when they are exposed to your brand. Brand perception is measured just like brand awareness, typically through consumer surveys where respondents specify which adjectives or values they associate with the brand. Brand perception is often measured among different segments and often against competing brands.

Which positive attributes does one brand 'own' with respect to another? Do consumers have the desired associations when the brand is mentioned?

Studies have shown that brand perception has a significant impact on whether we prefer Coca Cola or Pepsi. In a blind tasting, 50% of those surveyed preferred Pepsi over Coca Cola; however, if the test subjects were told which drink was Coca Cola, then three out of four suddenly preferred that. Measured on brain scans, it could also be seen that there were other brain sections activated when the subjects knew they were drinking Coca Cola, presumably due to their previous experiences and associations with the brand.[37]

Maturity level 2 – channel and campaign

In order to use performance analysis on a more instrumental level, it makes sense to zoom a little closer in on sales and the specific customer experience on every single channel. A channel-specific focus is a natural consequence of the classic organizational division, where the sales goals are broken down by unit and each channel has its independent campaigns and goals. This also enables optimization on an operational level.

Brand awareness and perception can also be measured on this level. It makes very good sense to measure brand perception after interaction with a specific campaign or channel in order to assess the effect on the brand.

Foot traffic

Before digital channels seriously took hold, in-store foot traffic was measured in stores, in conjunction with both determining a rental price at a specific address and analysing store performance. How large is the foot traffic on a specific day and how does this compare with sales? Sales per visiting customer is the conversion rate for retail stores. See more about conversion rates below.

Exposures, visits, page views, interactions and reach

In the belief that brand exposure creates greater brand familiarity and hopefully better perception, it makes sense to measure the number of exposures and interactions on the basis of a given effort or campaign on a given medium.

For banner advertising, the number of exposures is often tallied and billed by the thousand (CPM, or cost per mille), not least because consumers have generally stopped clicking banners. The basic assumption is that more exposure is better. Exposures can take on an extra quality dimension if you, as an advertiser, are certain that the exposed-to target group is the right one for your message. Exposure of the feminine hygiene brand Always to men would be a complete waste of money, for example.

Website visits were not always measured in the past, but today it is standard practice that scripts such as the one that Google Analytics offers be installed on all websites. Our guess is that you have it on your website; otherwise, there is no excuse for not immediately getting it done.

On social media the number of views of a given video or post is measured. Reach – i.e. the number of individuals the message has reached – is measured too. It is presumed that clicks and comments have a positive impact on brand awareness for those doing the clicking and commenting. In addition, clicks and comments have a positive influence on how likely the social media channel is to expose its content to multiple users, thus increasing its reach. Engagement is included in the ranking algorithms that are used; when it goes completely amok, we are talking about something going viral.

Today, virality is seldom achieved without the help of a large media budget. Digital business units often work intensely at optimizing customer flow, visits, views, interactions and reach, but unfortunate effects of these new metrics may arise and alienate the less digital part of the business. It can be difficult for a CEO to relate to whether a given action on the company's Facebook page is good or not, especially if no direct effect on sales can be shown.

Number of customers with marketing permission

Permissions are dealt with in detail in Chapter 1, but, in a nutshell, they include everything from Facebook 'likes' to Twitter, Instagram and LinkedIn followers to email and mobile device permissions.

Since the number of customers with a marketing permission has a direct impact on how many customers you can reach directly and without paying an advertising fee, naturally it's a metric that is often followed closely.

Email marketing campaigns are optimized by using data such as opening rate and click-through rate. This is because, to a certain extent, an opening or a click on an email is expected to lead to a purchase, or at least strengthen brand awareness and perception.

Basket size, conversion rate and lift

One of the classic success measures in commerce and e-commerce is basket size. How large is the average purchase? It is interesting to look at basket size when you are aiming to optimize cross-selling and up-selling. Can basket size be increased by something such as offering free shipping for purchases over €100, or by exposing customers to products related to those that are currently in the basket?

The conversion rate is the next thing you should look at, especially in e-commerce, where it is a completely standard metric to follow and optimize. The conversion rate is the percentage of visits that lead to a purchase. A 10% conversion rate means that one in ten website (or store) visits leads to a purchase. Website conversion rates generally range anywhere from 0.2% to 30%, depending on whether luxury goods or train tickets are being sold, and how close to a purchase decision customers are when they come to the site.

Conversion rates are often measured for each traffic source. How well does traffic convert when it comes from social media or from Google, for example? How well does the organic traffic from Google convert compared with the paid traffic? The immediate logical conclusion is to use more resources on the traffic sources that provide the best conversion rates. However, there are some pitfalls in thinking too single-mindedly about this; we will return to this notion later on.

Conversion rate optimization (CRO) is now a field in itself with advanced tools designed to help in improving it. Google Experiments is just one of them, along with Visual Website Optimizer, Optimizely, MixPanel and others. With all of these, the webmaster can set up real-time tests of which combinations of layout, text and images give the best conversion rates.

If the website's traffic volume is high enough, excellent results can be obtained by thorough, systematic and sustained optimization of the entire process from the first page view through to the final payment. Countless articles and books have been written about CRO, so we will not address it in detail. But we do think that organizing yourself around constantly optimizing solutions and measures is crucial to success. Read more about this in Chapter 6.

An interesting effect of online campaigns is the increase in measurable sales that a given campaign causes, even when the traffic does not come from the channel on which the campaign took place. For example, online retailer Saxo.com can measure a demonstrably increased effect on sales from the other traffic sources when it launches a campaign via email. This is called 'lift', which brings us to the next topic.

Multi-touch attribution

Multi-touch attribution is the art of attributing a share of the generated revenue not only to the source of the 'last click' but also across multiple touchpoints that the customer has had with the brand.

It makes good sense that the influence of various channels over time contributes to moving customers closer to a purchase decision. We rarely get data on every interaction a customer has with the brand, and it is not certain that every interaction will result in the customer visiting the website or even a second digital channel.

'Last click attribution' looks for the last thing the customer did (the last click) before they made a purchase and attributes all sales to the traffic source. Search terms that include your brand name thus typically have a relatively high conversion rate, but the actual purchase decision may have been made well beforehand, perhaps in connection with exposure from less measurable channels. Therefore, there is a pitfall in always optimizing in favour of the traffic source with the best conversion rate, so you should avoid doing this.

Google has partly met this challenge by being able to show multichannel funnels in Google Analytics. Google can provide a visualization of the overlap between the sources of traffic to a site that led to a purchase. However, this requires that the customer has been on the website several times, which is far from always the case. If you want to further increase the number of touchpoints you are including in your multi-touch attribution, it becomes increasingly hard to do so.

Sales models

Although there is a trend towards more and more communication channels being digitized and connected, we cannot determine with 100% certainty which channels an individual has been in contact with over time. For example, it is difficult to trace the influence of a physical advertisement placed at a bus stop, in a magazine, online or on TV.

To come closer to doing so, media agencies often develop advanced sales models, designed to give a more accurate picture of how individual channels contribute to sales. For instance, the actual performance of search marketing (e.g. Google AdWords) does not measure up to what appears in Google's or Yahoo's own reports. This is easily proven when a campaign running on TV and outdoor advertisements jointly result in a higher conversion rate for the traffic from search marketing – even though the AdWords remain unchanged. Needless to say, the TV commercials have had an effect, but it's not in Google's interest to emphasize this.

Although media agencies have faced accusations from digital agencies that sales models are created to sell more advertising, no one denies that brand exposure in all channels has an effect. This is connected to the idea of the long path to conversion, regardless of whether or not the channels are digital and measurable. Daniel Kahneman's book *Thinking, Fast and Slow* provides insights into how even the simplest exposures can form a bias for our actions.[38]

Sales models are advanced, but it is important to work with them when running a combination of offline and online advertising. Otherwise it can be difficult to get a picture of the individual channels' contribution to sales. However, very few companies have established sales models that can be used in daily or monthly optimizing. Nonetheless, the sales model is a useful tool for following up on a major effort or deciding your channel strategy and budget for paid media.

Maturity level 3 – customer-specific metrics

KPIs for sales and communication channels are useful for optimizing each organizational unit and individual (silo) channels. Sales modelling is a great tool for planning your media buying. But there are other metrics that put the customer at the centre of the analysis.

This is an approach that more and more retailers are adopting. For example, in its fourth-quarter 2017 earnings report, Nordstrom CFO Anne Bramman argued:

We're increasingly managing our business primarily through two brands, Nordstrom and Nordstrom Rack, rather than by channel. This includes migrating our metrics from a legacy store view to those that are more relevant to how customers are engaging with us.[39]

In the future, this is expected to become the norm for customer-centric companies.

Intake of new customers

In addition to measuring sales and the number of orders, you should also count the number of new customers you sell to. All studies show that it is easier and cheaper to sell to the same customers again than it is to recruit new customers.

If you do not have the data to determine whether or not customers are new or old, it might be a good idea to ask for it during registration in your customer club. We've seen that done for a large retailer: during its club's first year, a large portion of members stated that they were brand new customers. In order to properly measure the intake of new customers, you have to be able to recognize customers across all channels.

Customer churn (attrition)

Churn is a frequent KPI for companies with subscription-based business models. Churn is measured as the proportion of customers who have cancelled their subscription or most likely won't come back after a certain period of time. It is easiest to measure with subscription customers, for whom you have a recorded termination date. It is more difficult to measure in the retail sector, where companies work with repurchase propensities or probabilities. When the propensity of a repurchase within a year is calculated at 20% or lower, then it may be decided that this will be considered a customer loss, depending on the industry.

Customer lifetime value and customer loyalty

Customer lifetime value (CLV) is the net profit your company makes on a customer over time – for as long as the customer is a customer. Paul Farris and colleagues define CLV as follows in their book *Marketing Metrics*:

CLV: The present value of the future cash flows attributed to the customer during their entire relationship with the company.[40]

Therefore, it is an advanced function of turnover, costs, and, above all, time. CLV is fairly complex to calculate exactly, so many people work with approximations instead. See below.

Fred Reichheld, author of *The Ultimate Question* (more on him below), argues that word-of-mouth should be included when calculating CLV.[41] Therefore, customer value consists of:

- Revenues
  - Margin of all sales to the customer
  - Value of recommendations to others

- Expenditures
  - Cost of acquiring the customer
  - Cost of serving the customer
  - Cost of maintaining the customer relationship
  - Effect of customers talking negatively about the brand

CLV is interesting because it indicates how much money it is worth spending to acquire a new customer – the so-called customer acquisition cost (CAC). However, keep in mind that CAC depends on the assumption that future customers will be as good as the present ones, and it is only useful if the CEO and/or investors do not require quick growth in earnings here and now. Additionally, CAC can only be measured if the investment for acquiring customers allows for projections into the future.

CLV has often been used in industries and companies that are working with longer customer relationships. That is what omnichannel marketing is all about: working with customers and prospects over time. That is why CLV modelling is highly relevant.

For subscription-based companies, the ratio between CLV and CAC is often used in the valuation of a company. Many SaaS (software as a service) companies accept negative earnings as long as the CLV-to-CAC ratio is good. Klipfolio.com believes this ratio should ideally be somewhere around 3:1.[42]

Simple CLV variants

Because CLV can be difficult to calculate with precision and to a certain extent takes future profits as income up front, it can help to work with approximations or to simplify it. Often, the number of purchases and basket size over time (i.e. the value of sales per customer per year) are part of this. It is a somewhat easier function to calculate, since you only need the number of transactions and the average basket size.

Going back to Nordstrom's fourth-quarter earnings report, the company began to report on 'active customers' and 'sales per customer' where it used to report on 'sales per square foot' and 'sales per channel'.[43]

CLV-based segmentation

The behavioural segments you can derive from data analytics can be used again, with CLV measures overlaid, in your performance analysis. The point is that not all customers are of equal value, so it makes sense to continuously keep an eye on the size of each segment.

In this way, you can measure whether you are managing to move customers from the less profitable segments to the more profitable ones using omnichannel marketing.

A simplified overview could show how many customers have had both a large basket size and a high purchase frequency within the past month, how many have had a large basket size but low frequency, etc. It can be illustrated in a graph like this:

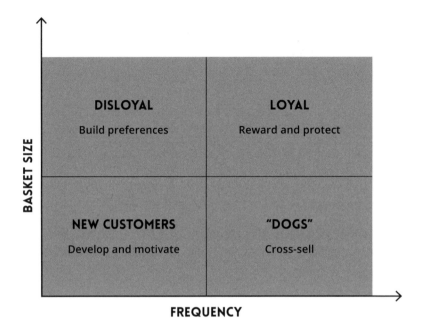

By continuously determining how many customers there are in each segment and tracking the movement among the segments, you will gain certainty regarding how the impact of your communication and service is developing.

The distribution is reminiscent of the traditional Boston Matrix[44], with dogs, cash cows, stars and question marks. The original model is intended to assess product potential, but the logic works fine for assessing your customers too.

Other customer-level metrics

There are several other metrics that could be included in this section. Most are components used in properly calculating CLV. However, it can also make good sense to track these separately, as they often influence CLV and will therefore be leading indicators of whether something is going one way or the other. In the following we comment briefly on some of the more important metrics.

Share of wallet

Share of wallet indicates the proportion of a customer's estimated budget within a specific category of services or products that is currently being spent in your business. For example, in B2B it can be calculated or estimated by looking at financial figures for the customer's size (e.g. turnover) as well as how much customers of the same size spend when all is going well.

Cost per lead

Cost per lead (CPL) is an expression of total cost across channels to attract a new lead or prospect. It could be booking a meeting or getting a new permission via email. Media consumption is typically included in this equation, but internal use of employees' time can also be factored in.

Customer acquisition cost

Customer acquisition cost (which was touched upon above) takes measuring success a step further than CPL. It is an expression of the total cost of acquiring a new customer, across channels. Just as for CPL, media consumption is typically included in this equation, and internal use of employees' time should also be factored in.

Cost of retention

Cost of retention is a summation of the expenditures needed to hold on to a given customer. The whole definition of what it means to hold on to a customer will of course be relevant in this context. It is easy to calculate in the case of a subscription business, but this becomes difficult for retail and thus isolated transactions. The calculation typically involves some form of probability that the customer will buy again within a certain time frame.

Strengths and weaknesses of customer-centric metrics

As with everything, there are pros and cons associated with the use of a particular framework over another. However, it is strongly recommended to define customer-centric KPIs rather than work with only channel- and campaign-specific KPIs.

Pros of using customer-centric metrics:
- provides a channel-independent picture of customer value
- provides input into how much it makes sense to spend on new customer acquisition
- together with control groups, can demonstrate the effect of new initiatives across channels.

Cons of using customer-centric metrics:
- CLV is difficult to calculate accurately
- it requires integration of multiple data sources in order to dig deeper into the causal links.

In reality, customer satisfaction is also included as a potential parameter in the calculation of several of the other customer-centric measurements. This brings us to the net promoter score (NPC), which does not just refer to behaviour-related data but involves actually asking customers what they think about your brand at certain times in the customer lifecycle.

Net promoter score

Hi, you've recently spoken with Jannie from Telenor. Based on that contact, how likely is it that you will recommend Telenor to a friend or colleague on a scale from 0 to 10, where 10 is very likely? Send your reply by texting back with one number. Sincerely, Telenor.

That is more or less the text a customer may receive from Telenor after having contacted its call centre. The customer can easily respond to the text message, it costs nothing, and the customer has a chance to express their frustration or praise.

Customers who answer the question can be divided into three categories:
- The least likely ambassadors are the detractors, those with a score from 0 to 6.
- Next are the passives, who are neither particularly satisfied nor negative.
- The brand's potential ambassadors are the promoters, with scores of 9 or 10.

The reason for asking about customers' willingness to recommend the brand is that, according to Fred Reichheld, author of *The Ultimate Question* and father of the NPS, the answer says far more about how valuable a customer is than does the level of satisfaction. Telenor is asking 'the ultimate question'.

Brand's net promoter score = **%Promoters** – **%Detractors**
To figure out a brand's NPS, the share of detractors is subtracted from that of promoters; therefore, a company could easily have a negative NPS. In that case, there would be more customers who would speak badly about the company than would recommend it. At an aggregated level, NPS is a strong indicator of the value of the customer base.

The value of customer recommendations

It's a rule of thumb that it takes four good statements to offset a negative one about a brand. So, in addition to promoters often being the most profitable customers (measured using purely economic indicators), their contribution to the word-of-mouth effect plays a major role in determining the overall CLV. In this way, detractors take on even less value and, at the same time, promoters create extra value because they speak so positively about the brand that they function as ambassadors and in that way help to bring in new customers. A promoter's CLV is considerably higher than that of a detractor.

This is illustrated in the model below from Fred Reichheld's book *The Ultimate Question*.[45]

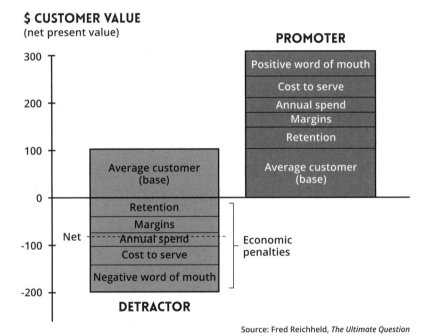

$ CUSTOMER VALUE
(net present value)

Source: Fred Reichheld, *The Ultimate Question*

Simple use – measuring brand perception

Just like Telenor, telecoms companies often use NPS to measure brand perception very broadly. By asking people – both customers and non-customers – whether they would recommend the brand over its competitors, these companies get a picture of the perception of competing brands. Are we more popular than the other brands?

Advanced use – life cycle, product, branch and employee

NPS should be measured on a more fine-grained level – for example, in relation to customers' place in the lifecycle, their connection to a specific branch or their use of a specific product. This allows the NPS score to be used to a greater extent in management decisions. For example, if you measure your customers' NPS right at the start of the customer relationship and compare it with when they have received a specific service or offer, you can get an indication of whether this service or offer is beneficial for the customer experience or the opposite. This can be valuable insight for when you are developing the customer experience.

Similarly, branches and even staff can be benchmarked against each other: are customers in this store more willing to recommend us than others? Talk to the staff and find out what they are doing differently. Let the less good branches and employees learn from the best and strengthen the customer experience in the stores all around.

Customer follow-up

Thank you for your rating! Although we are, of course, sorry about your experience. Help us to become better by answering a few more detailed questions. Click here to provide your input!

The customer's answer of a number between 0 and 10 is obviously valuable, but it is important to get a little behind the number and look at the cause. This can be done in a follow-up survey, e.g. via a link in a text message or email.

Pros and cons of NPS

NPS can be a great tool for measuring the effect of your customer-oriented initiatives. It is not very difficult to get started with, because of the myriad systems that can automate the process and aggregate the results in a sensible way.

If NPS is integrated into your organization's incentive structure, as a part of both management's and staff's bonuses, it can also help to create greater customer focus. This is a significant step forward from measuring in-store sales, provided that the item the customer was looking for is only available in the online store.

Moreover, NPS has the following advantages:
- It is easy to roll out. You do not need to integrate it into all possible (and impossible!) systems.
- It can give a quick indication of things that would otherwise take a long time to measure, e.g. loyalty.
- It enables the gathering of useful knowledge about what makes customers want to recommend your brand (or the opposite).
- It provides an opportunity to follow up on every dissatisfied customer and perhaps turn around their experience.

But:
- It may feel artificial asking customers to assess whether they would recommend a brand they do not really know. Instead, ask something else when you want to measure brand perception with loosely associated customers.
- It can feel hollow for customers if there is no follow-up of critical responses and explanations.
- It is *not* always a given that high NPS is linked to high CLV.
  - First, it is not certain that an indication will lead to an actual recommendation.
  - Second, certain products and services have attributes that mean NPS has no real impact on customer value, whether the answer is 10 or 5. For example, a product may simply be inherently unengaging, or it may be too bothersome to switch suppliers.

   ◦   Third, termination of a subscription may be due to a one-time event that cannot be predicted with respect to ambassador willingness.

Combining customer-centric and channel-specific measurements

Ideally you should combine the use of customer-centric (e.g. CLV and NPS) and channel-specific measurements. Realistically, there are probably not any companies that intend to stop using the built-in analytical tools that come with their email marketing, content management, conversion optimization and other tools. It is important to include the customer-centric KPIs in the equation and for them to remain the end goal of the optimization process. By doing so, you can guarantee that the optimization of each channel does not compromise the end goals of creating more profitable and satisfied customers.

The channel- and campaign-specific metrics will fortunately often prove to be leading indicators of what is going to happen with CLV. But it is important not to treat them in the same way, but to prioritize them according to which has the greatest impact on customer-centric metrics such as CLV. How do you find out what the priorities should be? Your data analytics should tell you, so go back to Chapter 3 if you are starting from scratch with this.

Predicting performance

As we mentioned in Chapter 3, some of the advanced, AI-based aspects of analytics can also be applied in performance analysis. You can move from KPIs to key performance predictors (KPPs), which give you forward-looking projections of where key metrics are likely to go. This can apply to channel- and campaign-specific metrics as well as customer-centric ones.

Unlike traditional forecasting techniques, KPPs are not simply an extrapolation of a 'headline' measure; they are built up by aggregating predictions made at the level of individual customers or cases (e.g. individual churn scores). This means that, like with KPIs, it is possible to drill down from the overall figure or trend to the segment or individual level, to understand more fully what is driving performance.

INCORPORATING PERFORMANCE ANALYSIS IN YOUR ORGANIZATION

Measuring the right KPIs and customer-centric metrics will not be useful if it is only happening in the marketing or sales department's own ivory towers. To really get the benefit of performance analysis, it has to become standard practice across your organization. So how do you get that to happen? In the following we will focus on various topics that are important for it to work:

- access
- degree of personalization
- benchmarks
- tools.

Access, visibility and understanding

Measurements are not something that should only be accessible to the finance and business intelligence departments. If the actual numbers are only available to top management, then it is only on that level that rational decisions will be made. Moreover, top management is universally known to act intuitively, on gut feelings, so the importance of them having access to updated reports on the state of things should not be overlooked.

Access for all to the right KPIs

Digital department managers are typically used to being able to keep track of how things are going with the digital channels. But that can easily become a little silo-like, in the sense that it is primarily the measurements for the digital channels that are kept track of, and not so much the customer-oriented KPIs that also involve the rest of the business.

This can also go the other way. For example, the retail side may solely look at the retail numbers (e.g. when the receipts are tallied up in the evening) and not at the general customer metrics. Value created by sending a customer over to the webshop or by accepting a returned item will thus be invisible for retail or perhaps even deducted from the store's numbers that day. This obviously does not help omnichannel and customer-centricity. Read more about channel conflicts in Chapter 6.

Visibility – show the KPIs and send the reports

If your employees can only see the fruits of half of their work, there is a high risk that they will end up prioritizing that half. For example, if it is cumbersome to submit measurements in specific areas (e.g. staff must log in and navigate to the right place) then in practice it may not get done. A common solution is to have a publicly visible presentation of the results and to send daily or weekly KPI reports to relevant stakeholders.

A gambling company in the Nordic countries had good KPIs that were accessible to everyone, at least in principle, because in practice employees could log on to the intranet and navigate to find them. Only this did not happen in practice, and all the value that was created via digital channels in the form of both new customers and self-service remained largely invisible. In contrast, it was highly visible when the phones rang in the customer service department and when customers visited the store. This resulted in a lot of extra focus being put on prioritizing resources and distorted the picture of where the value was created and on what the company should be focusing.

Just as it is important to make performance visible, it is also important to keep some nonessential measurements invisible. A large Danish company had a screen in its main office with a continually updated graph of the traffic numbers for its website compared with competitors' websites. It became something that was talked about, and, if the company was lagging behind its competitors, this was seen as bad. There was a greater chance that initiatives would be undertaken to get more traffic to the website. The company should instead have visualized a more central KPI, such as website goal attainment (e.g. how many people clicked on 'Find Store'). This would have made the talk around the water-cooler about quality rather than quantity.

Understanding metrics

New metrics are not necessarily self-explanatory. It can be complicated for a store or call centre employee to have to understand the whole omnichannel idea and the KPIs that go with it. It is therefore necessary to train and educate employees to understand, read and use the new KPIs. Where do employees see them, what do they mean and how can the employees see whether they are doing their job well or badly?

Degree of personalization

There are differences in the degree of motivation your employees get from looking at organizational and departmental measurements. If we assume that you have customer-centric KPIs for both the company and the department or unit, then it is of course more motivational for your staff to look at the figures that they have a direct possibility of influencing themselves.

At Telenor, each department has visible monitors with an overview of the KPIs relevant to it. In IT there are monitors hanging from the ceiling that continuously show response times on the website, uptime, etc. In sales, staff can see the day's results as well as the products topping the sales charts today. In the call centre, staff can see how many callers are in the queue at present and how satisfied the customers say they are at the end of each conversation.

Benchmarks

To give perspective to individual performance and help your employees determine whether they are doing their job well or badly, it is necessary to provide some perspective on the figures for the day, week or month. This can be done by comparing with – or benchmarking against – related figures.

Are we coming in above or below budget?

Probably the most frequently used benchmark is current performance in relation to the budget: are we above or below? However, it can be difficult to use this month's numbers for anything until the month is over.

Am I doing better than my colleagues?

Whether it's an individual against an individual or a branch against a branch, it may give some motivation for staff to be able to compare themselves with others in the company who share their objectives and responsibilities. Internal competition is one of the strongest means of activating personnel in retail chains. On the department level, you can create strong team spirit and unity by benchmarking in this way. On the individual level, you must be careful to ensure there is no suboptimization involved in people achieving their own numbers if it is also important for the company that employees cooperate.

Are we doing better than last week?

If you are working intensely to optimize and change your customer-facing processes, it may be interesting to compare the current period with a similar period within a shorter time horizon. For example, how are things going compared with last week, when you did things differently? Since you launched the app? Since launching the campaign?

This can provide good indications of whether things are going better, but there is always the danger that unforeseen factors in the outside world had an impact on customer behaviour, overshadowing the impact of the change you made. For example, the weather can have a significant influence on a visit to Disneyland – or ordinary shops, for that matter. The time of the month can also mean something. How long has it been since the customers were last paid?

Control groups

Control groups can help to isolate the effect of a new initiative. They are used in communication efforts where a group of customers are divided into two homogeneous groups, where one is the experimental group and the other is the control group. For example, the experimental group might be exposed to a quote on a specific product while the control group does not receive any communication about this offer. Statistically speaking, all factors other than the offer are therefore equal for the two groups. The impact of the offer is then compared between the two groups: how many redeemed the offer in each of them?

It can be difficult to use control groups in cases where it is not possible to isolate groups of customers. Often it will be difficult to use control groups for experiments in the physical world, but they are a fantastic tool for detecting effects of communication initiatives.

Any loyalty programmes should use control groups to determine the overall effect. The control group does not receive communications that are part of the programme, such as newsletters, invitations to events and deals. After a period, the economic performance of the two groups is calculated, which provides insight into how great an effect the loyalty programme has had overall.

Tools

In order to be able to highlight and explain relevant KPIs, it is necessary to have the proper tools, which must be capable of various things. Below we will review some important factors in choosing a system for performance analysis.

Data visualization

A picture says more than 1,000 spreadsheets. As we mentioned in Chapter 3, today's visualization tools go way beyond simple static charts and can be very powerful in helping you to spot patterns in data. A graphical representation of how well a campaign is going is significantly easier and more intuitive to decode than numbers in a spreadsheet.

Data integration

When you need to follow up on customer-centric KPIs, it soon becomes necessary to compare data from different channels. For example, it may be appropriate to compare campaign data from your email system with transaction data from the ERP (enterprise resource planning) system that the stores' points of sale feed into. Otherwise, how can you measure the sales volume your newsletter generates in the stores?

Typically, the behavioural data from your website, customer marketing platform, email system, app, CRM (customer relationship management) system, social media, and the cash registry or ERP system are integrated in order to visualize the customer-centric KPIs. But let's take one thing at a time.

Send reports regularly and automatically via email

Apart from displaying always updated performance dashboards, it is an advantage if your system for performance analysis can send regular reports to the appropriate stakeholders.

Interactivity and performance

It is one thing to show the state of things here and now. It can be hard enough to define what metrics you want your employees to be persistently exposed to and to make it happen. The tool you are looking for must have good functionality for visualizing performance and presenting numbers in tailor-made dashboards that can be displayed either on big screens around the organization or in individualized form on employees' computers.

But, when the figures are not as expected, it becomes important to be able to view them over time in order to determine the direction of the figures and, not least, to be able to delve deeper into why the overall figures are not moving as expected. Which underlying leading indicator is making that particular KPI behave undesirably?

This function is substantially different from just providing a display and is typically not something that will be done on the monitors in communal areas. It must be possible to dive into the numbers from the desktop by folding out a number to see what is hiding behind it. In order to work with it, such an operation should not take too much time. A second or two's wait is fine; however, if five minutes or more go by each time a question must be answered, the tool loses its impact and thus its value.

The same tools as for data analytics?

As the underlying information on your performance is data, the whole range of analytics and AI tools and capabilities described in Chapter 3 could in principle be applied to it. Analytically advanced organizations should be capable of using algorithms to help automatically discover significant patterns in performance data.

For many companies, however, this could be a case of using a sledgehammer to crack open a nut. Not all 'information consumers' need to be using the same systems to view, explore and analyse data. As long as the data foundation is the same, one set of systems could easily be used for data analytics and another for viewing KPIs through visualizations or dashboards.

PITFALLS OF BEING NUMBERS-ORIENTED

The danger in focusing too much on purely numerical targets is that the excessive focus on the target goes beyond the desired effect. It can also create a working environment where there is no motivation or space to help each other.

Another danger is that the numbers do not capture the essence of the organization. For example, if your customer experience is highly dependent on how satisfied your employees are, which is the case in the consultancy industry, focusing too much on the monthly budgets could result in an unpleasant workplace. This can rebound in the form of disgruntled employees and then disgruntled customers, thus making it even harder to hit the numbers in the following month.

Performance analysis cannot replace leadership

It is important to stress that good performance analysis cannot replace good leadership. If no one understands the company's purpose and buys into the vision of the great cathedral they are helping to build, then performance analysis will not be able to save the company. Management that inspires, motivates and creates a working environment that is enjoyable for all is still necessary. So, essentially, there is a great difference between 'management' and 'leadership'.

A MEASUREMENT CULTURE

In order to achieve what we call a 'measurement culture', you need to succeed at several things:

- You need to find the right customer-centric KPIs and determine which other metrics serve as the leading indicators for these.
- You should implement a visualization tool that displays the right KPIs for the right employees. The difference the individuals' efforts make must be visible.
- Your employees must be trained to constantly optimize their efforts based on the continuous feedback they receive from their manager and the measurements that are within reach.

These are the things that performance analysis is all about: most people in your organization constantly make decisions and they should do so on the basis of factual insight into the state of current performance and the development thereof. If they also have the ability to examine the figures in closer detail when there is something they do not understand or would like to improve, then you've come a long way.

MATURITY IN PERFORMANCE ANALYSIS

Customer metrics
Real time
Measurement culture
Key performance predictors

Channel and campaign
Attribution modelling
Channel and organizational
unit accountability

Turnover – market share
Brand awareness and perception
C-level accountability
Quarterly reporting

Highest maturity level

Companies with mature performance analysis have established a goal hierarchy via thorough data analytics. In this way, channel- and campaign-specific metrics function as weighted leading indicators for customer-centric KPIs. Also, AI can be used to predict the most likely evolution of these in KPPs. All company employees know the goals of their function; they also have easy access to their function's status and the ability to make their own data-based decisions. When new customer-related initiatives are launched, control groups are used to assess their relative effects, to the extent possible.

Middle maturity level

Companies of mid-maturity in performance analysis adopt a structured approach to measuring and optimizing the specific sales and marketing channels that are often reflected in specific physical and digital departments. Measurement is done using a before-and-after method, and there is no well-established hierarchy for which measurements are the best leading indicators of the company's long-term success. The brightest of these companies will work with sales modelling in order to identify the extent to which advertising on different channels contributes to sales.

Lowest maturity level

The companies that are the least mature in performance analysis primarily measure anonymized sales figures, earnings and market share. On the brand and marketing side, they concentrate on brand awareness and brand perception. It is generally only management that gets quarterly and at best monthly figures on the company's financial and brand-related results.

Remember that you can take our test based on the Omnichannel Hexagon and find your company's omnichannel maturity level at:

OMNICHANNELFORBUSINESS.ORG

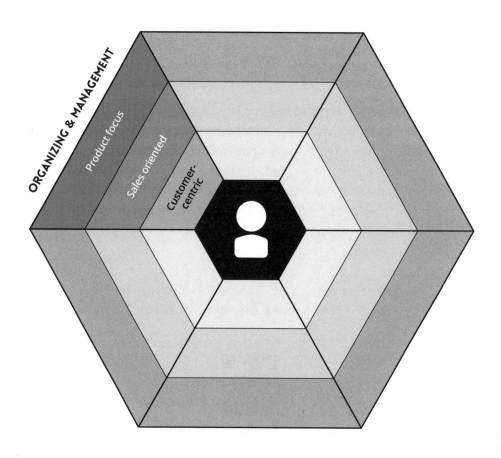

6

ORGANIZING & MANAGEMENT

Organization and incentive structures must support the best possible service for customers across channels. Otherwise, individual agendas and objectives will quickly block your way towards great omnichannel customer experiences. Your organization must also possess the right skills and the right tools.

On Chloé's first day as a beauty advisor with Sephora, she attended the Sephora University in Paris. There she learned about the 'Sephora Attitude', skin care, makeup and perfume. It seemed like Sephora had a special way of being customer-centric.

The main part of the training covered how Sephora connects with its customers, and which tools and techniques are used to achieve this. For starters, there were the digital in-store tools. The Sephora app helped to guide customers to stores and to specific products on the shelves and it also sent notifications of daily promotions. Customers could try on makeup by using the Virtual (Makeup) Artist, which applied makeup filters in real time.

Then there was the Beauty Insider loyalty programme, which was a community of customers who shared an interest in looking good. Through the community, customers were able to match with fellow members who shared their skin type or hair style and tips on what works best. Customers also had their virtual Beauty Bag, where they could see all their favourite products and past purchases, making it extremely easy to replenish products.

Most of the usual tasks of a sales associate were so well supported by technology and self-service tools that Chloé could concentrate more on helping customers to find the right look and use the tools to guide them along the way.[46]

IT'S NOT ALL ABOUT TECHNOLOGY

I t takes more than smart technology to make omnichannel a reality in your business. Technology is not some magic fairy dust that you can sprinkle over your organization and suddenly expect your employees to use it with the desired result. If you want to succeed with omnichannel and AI, it is important not to treat them as isolated projects.

Transitioning into omnichannel marketing should be firmly anchored, and it involves change across the entire organization. Omnichannel is a constantly developing area, and it's hard to remain at the forefront and know in advance what will work and what will not. You'd better get started before your business is disrupted by Amazon, JD.com, Alibaba.com or some other company we do not yet know.

What is needed from the organization?

The question is, how will your business succeed in creating great omnichannel customer experiences? In this chapter, we have gathered together some key topics about working with omnichannel in your organization:

- CEO support and anchorage
- collaboration between departments
- realigning incentive structures
- the global marketing organization
- instilling an omnichannel culture
- a new operating model for omnichannel marketing
- omnichannel skills and resources needed.

GETTING CEO SUPPORT IS CRUCIAL

You will need your team, but more importantly you'll need help from across the organization. You could take it upon yourself to convince other departments, but, even if they understand your motives for business success and believe that an omnichannel transformation is necessary, they will still be stuck in a department and a role that are defined by yesterday's standards. The old standards will still be defining what they get paid for, what their targets are and what will ultimately result in their personal financial and professional success. So, as with all organizational changes, this is something that has to come from the top – but changing the mind of the CEO is not something that happens overnight. An omnichannel transformation is the right thing to do, but that doesn't mean that it will be first in line in the CEO's priorities for what needs to happen today.

Align with your CEO's goals

Show a true business understanding that is beyond marketing. Remember that long-term business success includes being relevant to as many customers as possible. So, make sure your CEO knows that you are aware of this. Accept the fact that you'll have to keep doing traditional marketing along with all the new stuff for at least a few more years and avoid being too narrowly focused on the personalized marketing agenda.

Gather a guiding coalition

Who in the management team is already supporting this agenda? Using data to optimize response rates, customer engagement, sales and other parts of a business is not a new idea. Try to look for isolated examples where smart people have done the right thing regardless of how supportive the management was or wasn't. Chances are they felt they didn't get enough credit for this and they didn't have the power and impact to implement and sustain the potential benefits. These are the people you need back-up from.

The first part of working together is establishing a common language and vocabulary. All too often, understanding is lost in translation as different departments use their own jargon. A way to start overcoming this barrier is to do the omnichannel benchmark survey with your colleagues (see the link at the end of this chapter). Discussing how to answer the different questions will create a common understanding of the most important terms and set you on a path towards understanding and a common direction.

Have your CEO read this book

The introduction and this chapter, especially, will lead to some degree of shared understanding. You could also introduce your CEO to the omnichannel benchmark tool and the results you and your guiding coalition ended up with. Sometimes CEOs are more concerned about the state of their immediate competitive peers than the threats of Alibaba.com and JD.com.

Get appointed as the change agent

Someone has to drive the omnichannel transformation, and if you have already gathered the guiding coalition and convinced your CEO, it should be a simple task to get a formal appointment as the change agent. If this is not a simple task, it could be because your organization needs to fix more fundamental issues that currently threaten the survival of your business in the short term. Essentially, the way a project such as this is handled can be crucial for future omnichannel endeavours.

Clarify the support you'll need

This chapter will clarify the kinds of questions and deliverables you will need support on from the various parts of the organization. Make it clear how the result should look and what you need from others to achieve this. Explain what stands in the way – most likely, you'll uncover issues with existing department goals and job descriptions, and their corresponding incentive structures and reward schemes. More about this later.

Realign objectives and incentives

Some of your guiding coalition may be the ones responsible for pitching in on an omnichannel transformation. But they won't do so if it means they'll miss their targets and get paid less. So, for these people and especially those who are not on board, your CEO needs to realign targets and incentive structures so that they do not block the deliverables needed for the omnichannel transformation. This obviously cannot be done overnight, so be patient and get acceptance from other parts of the C-suite. Once the above is in place, it's change (management) as usual until you are through the omnichannel transformation.[47]

COLLABORATION – WHO DOES WHAT?

What role are you in? As discussed earlier, omnichannel transformation needs to be anchored with the CEO, but the leading change agent is not likely to be this person. So, who will grab the wheel? According to a 2018 Accenture study[48] by Forrester, the C-suite alphabet soup (CEO, CMO, CXO, CAO, COO, CIO, CFO, etc.) in its own indirect way stresses the importance of collaboration between departments. Forrester even suggests the intermediary title 'chief collaboration officer' – not as a real title but inferring that whomever takes the lead will have to be an expert collaborator.

Will marketing take the steering wheel?

The shift from digital obsession to customer obsession in the B2C (business-to-consumer) world means that the marketing department and the CMO (chief marketing officer) are well positioned to take the wheel in the omnichannel transformation. In fact, according to the Forrester study cited above, 90% of respondents saw the CMO as the connective tissue between the different lines of business.

There are three key points that make this plausible:
1. Marketing activities have moved from being centred on brand and advertising to being centred on customers.
2. Marketing is the central function that has the greatest reach and number of interactions with customers on a daily basis.
3. The marketing function has been heavily infused with and is thus accustomed to a multitude of digital tools.

Given the three points above, it makes sense for marketing departments to lead companies from a digital obsession into real omnichannel.

The Boston Consulting Group voices the same view in an article from May 2017:

> For incumbents to defend – and expand – share, they need to reimagine their business with an individualized value proposition at the core, merging physical and digital experiences to deepen their customer connections. They need to put brand individualization at the forefront of their strategy agenda to influence everything that they do, including marketing, operations, merchandising, and product development.[49]

But it doesn't have to be the CMO taking charge. Other constellations are possible, but they all seem to unite and build upon the principles behind digital customer interaction.

Take, for instance, Sephora. An interview with the online magazine *Glossy* in April 2018[50] covers how Sephora has combined its in-store, digital and customer service efforts under one roof. This is all headed by Mary Beth Laughton, who is executive vice president (EVP) of omni retail at Sephora, having previously been senior vice president (SVP) of digital. Sephora is progressing from a digital transformation to an omnichannel transformation.

In the case of Sephora, some of the previous core marketing tasks, such as branding and advertising, are now handled by an SVP of marketing and brand. These are still important tasks, but not enough for the person carrying them out to be in the driving seat of this transformation.

The new titles

EVP of omni retail, chief customer officer and chief commercial officer are all new titles indicating that there is a unification of responsibility underway, along with a desire to overcome internal barriers and break down silos that jeopardize customer loyalty in favour of suboptimizing each sales and marketing channel on its own. These titles often carry a profit and loss responsibility, which saves them from being 'kings without a crown'. They have responsibility for both earning and spending money – the money to back up omnichannel and the responsibility if it doesn't work as intended. This isn't necessarily the case with positions such as chief experience officer and chief digital officer, which can lose influence if they don't have a clear budget and a clear mandate.

Whether or not the CMO will grow into one of these titles or live in harmony collaborating with the rest of the C-gang we'll leave up to you, the reader and the future to tell. For the remainder of this chapter, we'll simply refer to the CMO as the one in the driving seat.

Finally, although analytics and AI are key parts of succeeding with an omnichannel transformation, it is less likely that the chief analytics officer will be the one who takes charge of the omnichannel transformation.

The need for collaboration across functions

The CMO will need to take care of traditional marketing as well as omnichannel marketing and run the transformation at the same time. But what is required from other departments?

Collaborating with sales

For the Omnichannel Hexagon to work, you will need a great deal of help from the sales departments, which of course can take many different shapes. If you are in a bricks-and-mortar retail business, then sales is often a synonym for retail. If you are in a pureplay e-commerce business, then sales is often a synonym for e-commerce and the silo mentality will be easier to break down. In B2B (business-to-business, e.g. a manufacturing company), things can swing two ways. You are either in a volume-based business or in a business with really complex sales where personal relationships matter a lot.

In this book we focus on volume-based business, regardless of whether it is B2B or B2C. So, even though an account manager can benefit greatly from insights and data collected from digital engagement in their conversations with clients and potential clients – in many similar ways to omnichannel – we chose not to go too much into this but leave it to the latest literature on so-called account-based marketing.

Assuming that you are in a volume-based business, you are either directly or indirectly dealing with consumers.

Getting support from B2C sales (retail) involves:
- signing up and identifying customers in-store
- implementing digital tools
- ongoing training of personnel
- promoting, instilling and rewarding an omnichannel culture.

Getting support from B2B sales involves:
- using sales to promote digital tools that help resellers (and possibly collect data)
- doing deals with retailers and resellers to get data from end customers.

If you fail to get sales to subscribe to your omnichannel transformation, you'll be in for a treat of the classic channel conflicts. Studies do show that omnichannel shoppers' spending increases with the number of channels they use to interact with brands.[51] However, without proper rethinking of incentives and reward schemes, store managers will often perceive e-commerce as their worst competitor and thus won't have their personnel sign up customers, ask for membership, use the new digital tools in-store, receive return items with a smile (and get the up-sell), etc.

Collaborating with IT

If instability of core business platforms (inaccurate inventory numbers in retail, dropped calls in telecoms, etc) is still a problem, then it will take time before the marketing activity can make any difference within omnichannel. Similarly, if you would like the IT department to support building and maintaining advanced systems, you will most likely be placed in line behind projects concerned with fixing the basics. It can take time. So be patient.

If you are in a company that owns brick-and-mortar stores, then you'll need the IT department to support the building, deployment and maintenance of new hardware that goes into the stores. This accounts for things such as:

- in-store kiosks where customers can check store availability of items and self-service the ordering of these (in-store e-commerce)
- magic mirrors for use in dressing rooms, as in the case of the Libert'aime store in Shanghai (see Chapter 1), where, after having signed up for the loyalty programme, customers can take photos of themselves wearing jewellery and share these with their friends
- extended point-of-sale (POS) functionality so sales associates can look up individual customers and see their previous history, wishlists, items left in their online shopping basket and most likely future purchases

- 'clientelling' apps, which liberate sales associates by integrating all detailed POS and customer information into a portable device that can be used at any place in the store and not at a separate desk
- in-store Wi-Fi and beacons, in order to be able to recognize customers in-store.

Apart from building and maintaining this extra omnichannel-related hardware, there is also the task of managing the customer data. Historically, the IT department's primary tasks used to be (and probably still are) reporting sales numbers to the chief financial officer. But IT didn't necessarily ask questions about customer data. Although GDPR (the EU's General Data Protection Regulation) was originally perceived as a big potential barrier for omnichannel marketing in Europe and for any company that does business in Europe, it has proved to be a great win since IT departments have now been forced to take customer data seriously and put it into ordered databases in order to comply with public regulations. This more than makes up for the few thousand unengaged customer records that had to be deleted because no one remembered which consent they had agreed to (if any, ever).

The ownership of marketing technology

Today, marketing departments often have ownership of cloud-based marketing technology (martech) platforms (often delivered through the cloud like 'software as a service'). In these platforms' sales materials, it is often portrayed as an advantage that the marketing department does not need to involve IT (much) to get going. These platforms need not be dangerous for either security or stability, but, if the IT department is responsible for these areas, the marketing department must respect that IT will be involved and consulted when choosing the systems and making customer data storage and integration decisions.

Getting insights from analytics

As described in Chapter 3, it is important that the IT (or business intelligence) department is not only reactively reporting on sales figures but is also equipped (tools, data), staffed (resources) and skilled (competent) enough to deliver both high-level reports and data visualizations. A dedicated analytics department should implement ongoing propensity scoring and clustering of end customers in terms of who they are, what kind of people they are and with which kinds of behaviour and characteristics, what they are most likely interested in, what they will most likely do or buy, what the chances are that they are going to leave you, and (if so) whether they might be worth saving (and possible to save).

Analytics is not done entirely for the sake of marketing. With a certain level of maturity and sufficient resources, it can be a good idea to have a dedicated CRM (customer relationship management) analyst, whether organizationally they belong to the marketing or the analytics department.

Collaborating with research and development

Liaison with research and development (R&D) is mainly relevant for manufacturing companies that primarily deal indirectly with their customers. It is possible to build data collection into the core of a product, by integrating RFID (radio-frequency identification) chips or similar into the woven fabric of the product or into the digital core of an electrical product (hearing aids, cars, e-readers, tablets, active loudspeakers, software and even adult diapers). It is paramount to omnichannel success that R&D does not have its own closed ecosystem around these data, but that it in fact collaborates with marketing, CRM and analytics about leveraging this technological advantage.

Collaborating with human resources

You'll need human resources (HR) to help educate and train existing employees in the overall concepts of omnichannel as well as the specific tasks that are affected by the new normal. Omnichannel skills and competencies are also important when recruiting new employees or designing new organizational structures spanning across previous departments in the company. HR is also a key stakeholder when it comes to redesigning incentive structures and compensation packages that suit the new omnichannel agenda.

REALIGNING INCENTIVE STRUCTURES

It is important that people not only understand but are also incentivized to support the omnichannel transformation. If this is not handled properly, they may even be economically incentivized to work against it. This has to change.

Incentives do not just affect individual employees and what they need to achieve. In the early years of the 2000s, when customers didn't have a great many bidirectional communication channels to switch between, it made good sense to break down the company's overall target into sub-targets for each organizational unit and link these to personal incentives for the responsible employee. Every region, regional manager, district manager and store manager had their sales and cost targets, and every salesperson had their sales targets.

With the development of e-commerce, it seemed natural to establish a unit for it, with its own revenue and cost targets. Thus came about the previously mentioned channel conflict between physical stores and the webshop. Furthermore, if e-commerce was placed under the marketing department, from an organizational standpoint, it could create an overall conflict between sales and e-commerce, which from the customer's point of view seems quite paradoxical.

Individual or joint incentives

Incentives can be either individual or joint. For example, there may be a common reward for achieving a common goal, which should foster cooperation and provide a sense of community. Shared rewards are best suited to complex tasks that require the close cooperation of several people, while individual incentives lend themselves more to tasks to be handled by an individual, e.g. a meeting booker getting €200 for each meeting. It is evident that individual incentives are not conducive to cooperation within a common unit.

Incentives do not always follow the organizational structure. Although e-commerce, for historical reasons, might still be placed under marketing rather than sales, it is possible for a portion of the sales director's bonus to depend on sales via e-commerce.

Incentives should reflect customer-centric KPIs

In order for incentives to be realized, it is necessary to conduct ongoing performance analysis on the company, departmental and individual employee levels. As discussed in Chapter 5, targets and incentives should reflect what is best for long-term customer profitability and not unconsciously motivate suboptimization within each sales channel.

Even when individual employees understand that a given action would be the right thing for a customer and for the company, in truth they often choose to do it because they know it will incur a bonus or be brought up in their appraisal interview. Tasks that do not count towards targets but serve

the common good will be taken care of after the other tasks –
so, in busy times, not at all.

But why haven't the incentives been restructured already?

The answer is simple: because it is hard to do.

It is hard to change the job targets and bonus schemes of a
department if there is no incentive for the boss to do so. Why
would your sales director urge store employees to send customers over to 'marketing's webshop'? For this reason, top
management must decide to do away with silo thinking and
put the customer in the centre.

Once the will is there, there is still a way to go since appraisal
interviews only occur once a year and call centre, in-store and
franchise store employees may already have old-style bonus
schemes in place. It requires hard work to restructure incentives,
but it is necessary if you want to succeed with omnichannel.

Are incentive structure problems a transitional problem?

In a roundtable session arranged by the authors for debating
the omnichannel hexagon, Per Rasmussen, CEO of eCapacity
(a Copenhagen- and London-based e-commerce consultancy)
claimed that challenges related to incentive structures and
channel conflicts should be a transitional phenomenon that
may seem rather insurmountable at present. But, in the future,
customer-centric incentive structures will be seen as something natural that need not even be explained to new recruits,
since such incentive structures will have been present where
they came from. However, we believe there is still a way to go
to reach this point.

Incentive structures in stores

It is critical to revise the way that numbers are tallied and incentives are set up in stores, in order to increase the chances of gathering permissions and creating good customer experiences. First, it must be made clear to the store employees – management as well – that it really is their job to help customers buy items online and accept returns of items bought online. A customer who is returning a gift that is not in the store's inventory has likely come to that store because it is close by. If their attempt to return the item results in a bad experience, the customer may not come back to that store again.

Second, store staff should not be penalized for exchanging online items. If the store or its staff have specific targets for revenue and expenditure, online sales from the store should count fully in the store's turnover, and the return of an item bought online should not cost the store anything in the accounts (unless, of course, the full value of this sale was attributed to the store in the first place).

Third, stores should be happy to get traffic. You should therefore use both anecdotes and hard numbers to illustrate that every customer who shows up in the store wanting to pick up an online order or exchange an item represents a potential up-sell.

Fourth, the introduction of click and collect, i.e. in-store pick-up of items purchased online, provides an understanding of how online sales help to generate in-store sales. This can be achieved by integrating online behavioural data at the POS or by store managers sending their own personalized newsletters to customers in the immediate area with information on local events and promotions. According to a study from 2017 by JDA and Centiro, almost a quarter (24%) of European adults who used click and collect bought another item while picking up their order.[52]

Michael Relich, the chief operating officer of the US-based furniture company Crate & Barrel, supports the realignment of incentive structures for in-store personnel:

Retailers need to align incentives around omni-channel. Too often, stores are given credit for stores sales and ecom is incentivized on ecom sales, which lead[s] to less of a seamless experience. Consumers don't care about how you are organized. You got to make it seamless.[53]

Similarly, Williams Sonoma EVP Patrick Connolly says:

Employees are rewarded for online purchases they initiate, and returns are appropriated to the right channels to avoid penalizing them for returns of online merchandise. The channel-agnostic philosophy has roots at the enterprise, since stores were encouraged to distribute catalogues without fear of cannibalizing their segment.[54]

Incentives are meant to encourage certain behaviour and can be both soft and hard. Soft incentives are merely a reflection of what is expected of employees, while hard incentives have a direct impact on employee compensation, typically in the form of bonuses paid to individual workers.

Incentives for the digital marketing team

Digital marketing teams also need to be measured against the new structure. Just like all the other departments, their incentive structures must be realigned and they will need retraining. They must build the digital solutions and digital marketing in a way that also benefits the brick-and-mortar stores, such as by driving foot traffic to the nearest stores, displaying stores' current product inventory, or inviting (or enabling the retail manager to invite) customers to local events.

Silos within marketing

Even within marketing departments, silos can appear. This is especially true if you operate with dedicated communication channel managers, but it can also be a consequence of the sheer volume of activity. You should be aware that the tools used on each of the channels can, in themselves, help to reinforce silos, with regard to skills, data and even language use (i.e. different metrics). Misaligned incentive structures can increase this tendency further.

Thus, internal knowledge-sharing and collaboration must be priorities. If the members of the marketing department cannot work together, then what does that say for the prospect of cooperation with the rest of the organization? Then how will you succeed at omnichannel?

THE GLOBAL MARKETING ORGANIZATION

In global companies, each region or country usually has its own marketing function and often digital competence as well. Regions that are very large in terms of sales often hold a lot of power and can be quite autonomous. This implies the risk that the role of global marketing may be limited to developing the central brand and ensuring that it is used uniformly across countries and regions, i.e. wielding brand governance.

On the digital front, without a considerable budget and personnel, global marketing can be reduced to producing digital tools that are primarily used by the regions that do not have large enough departments or budgets to do it themselves. That is, global marketing can become more of a lowest common denominator than a driver of innovation.

It is important to take steps to avoid your marketing department's potential being curtailed in this way.

How to do omnichannel glocally

In order to have success with omnichannel marketing and AI, power and initiative need to be centralized while still leaving room for regions to localize central initiatives and hold their own events.

In this way, local markets can mainly work with content and events, whereas special skills such as digital development (web, app), automation and analytics are best handled centrally, where it is possible to achieve critical mass and create and sustain a specialist community that is less dependent on specific people. For data analytics, localization of predictive models may also be needed, but, instead of outsourcing this to the individual regions, it should be handled by the central organization with input from the local markets on how consumers behave in their part of the world. Keep in mind, though, that it takes at least double the time and resources to develop materials that are suitable for use across cultures, so make sure the central department is well funded.

Many companies take a regional approach by dividing the world into groups of countries – e.g. North America, Latin America, Europe (sometimes including the Middle East and Africa), South East Asia or even just APAC (Asia Pacific), or similar. For some companies this can enable the right trade-off between centralization and time to market.

OMNICHANNEL CULTURE

It is not enough to have the organization, incentives and skills in place, if your corporate culture does not support omnichannel work. Chapter 5 provided a great example of how cultural change can be achieved. Rasmus, a digital sales manager for Telenor, chose to pursue the omnichannel initiative of 'reserve & collect' (i.e. allowing customers to reserve an item and then pay for it when they collect it from the store), even though this was directly in conflict with the way the company traditionally measured and attributed sales. It meant moving the conversion to the store, which strictly speaking was out of Rasmus's area of responsibility. The fact that Rasmus had the idea in the first place and also had the confidence that incentives would be changed if the experiment worked is proof that Telenor has been successful in implementing an omnichannel culture.

In *Corporate Cultures*, authors Terrence Deal and Allan Kennedy describe corporate culture as "the way things are done here in the company".[55] The culture consists of all the written and unwritten rules, as well as the company's guiding values and principles. If employees are in any doubt about what needs to be done, they will unconsciously draw on the corporate culture to find a basis for their decision.

Omnichannel understanding

Your employees must understand that they are part of a customer-oriented company. Even with incentives and organizational units in place, new employees must quickly get the feeling that, in your company, staff work with the customer in focus, when they produce, when they communicate and when they serve.

Amazon is a good example of a company that has built customer focus deeply into its culture. As early as 1997, Amazon's CEO, Jeff Bezos, said the following, which illustrates how the company is 100% committed to a customer focus:

We're not competitor-obsessed, we're customer-obsessed. We start with the customer and we work backwards. [56]

It is important that every employee has a sense of the six disciplines of omnichannel marketing and understands that they need to recognize customers across channels, ask for permissions, collect data, and use both data and insights derived from it to improve service and communication for every single customer. If this doesn't happen, then expensive IT investments can easily end up unused and results will fall behind.

Understanding customer data

A significant part of incorporating omnichannel in a company consists of working with customer data. Therefore, your employees should understand what it means to be data driven and, first and foremost, what it means for their own work tasks.

In the digital department, the managers of the different channels must be able to read and understand data. They have to be able to work with databases and data correlations, know the routines for data importing and exporting, know the conventions for naming, know where the APIs (application program interfaces) are, etc. This can be new territory and difficult to access for employees with a traditional, more brochure-oriented approach to marketing.

Even when conducting mass-media campaigns, it is important that employees understand how to use data. Insights from customer data can indeed be used in creative concepts.

Permission and data collection should also be included in the campaign tactics, so that the attention of interested customers doesn't have to be re-purchased later but they can be reached with a personalized message through owned media next time.

Experimental approach

In a world where technological development moves quickly, what the next big thing will be cannot be determined in advance. Even the trend spotters have difficulty keeping up and predicting the coming year's trends.

In order to stay ahead of the competition, companies must experiment with new ways of doing things. It is a matter of launching new projects and keeping an open mind about the existing solutions while continuing to optimize without risking the entire business. We are seeing this trend on the part of Alibaba, Amazon, Google and many of the other major players, which constantly run 'beta' projects to test what the next big thing might be.

Your employees must be encouraged to experiment and be rewarded for doing so. They should not be punished for trying things that are not at first successful. Experimentation creates knowledge, and, when it is shared, it leads to new ideas. Although it is nice to have a bullet-proof business case for every project, insisting that this is the case can easily mean that new initiatives will be choked by bureaucracy and competitors will have taken the lead in the meantime, in the worst case getting good publicity for being innovative.

Work hard, play hard

Deal and Kennedy divide corporate cultures into a 2×2 matrix with feedback speed (i.e. how quick the company is to learn the lessons of new measures) on one axis and risk tolerance (i.e. how much is staked on each initiative) on the other.[57]

In relation to Deal and Kennedy's four archetypes of corporate culture, the ideal omnichannel culture most closely resembles is what they call "work hard, play hard": experiment frequently, risk a little bit every time and constantly learn from the experiments you carry out.

Source: https://www.mindtools.com/pages/article/newSTR_86.htm

Instilling the omnichannel culture

Since omnichannel and customer-centricity are not yet the norm, an omnichannel transformation will require both intense internal marketing and training. It will also need an ongoing effort to keep all existing and especially new employees up to date.

First, make sure that all employees are aware that the company is a customer-centric, omnichannel one and what that means for the customer experience, for the employees and for the employees' daily tasks and targets. Treat this as a normal (yet internal) marketing campaign. Conceptualize it, give it a name, produce key assets and collateral (such as descriptive videos, interviews and narratives), and distribute these. Roadshows in various regions, stores and departments may be needed as well.

Second, make sure that personnel receive practical training in performing the new tasks. For instance, CRM employees will need training in how to operate new marketing technology and sales associates will need to be trained in operating in-store kiosks, clienteling apps, magic mirrors, etc. As a source of inspiration, we consider Sephora[58] a great example of how training is approached as a focus area in omnichannel.

Third, visualize the difference that omnichannel makes by providing all departments and employees with easy and immediate access to dashboards displaying the current status of customer-oriented and omnichannel metrics and how the teams are contributing to business success.

OPERATING MODEL

When the decision has been made to embark on an omnichannel transformation, first decide what the journey will look like. Then ask how you plan to support that journey.

NEW CUSTOMER JOURNEY(S)

SUPPORTING TASKS

Manual tasks	Automated tasks
Skills and training	Functionality and features
Culture and incentives	Platforms

Supporting it will require performing new tasks. Some of these will be handled by your staff manually (i.e. signing up an in-store customer for the loyalty programme) whereas others will be automated (i.e. alerting a customer that a requested item is back in stock). Manual tasks require your employees to have the skills to perform them, so you have to train them. On a more profound level, employees need the motivation to carry out these tasks – this is rooted in the omnichannel culture and the right alignment of incentives.

Automated tasks must be set up using the functionality and features of the marketing technology stack. Sometimes these platforms do not have the required functionality, so this has to be developed or perhaps the platform needs to be changed.

When the future omnichannel customer journey is envisioned, it makes sense to look at what work needs to be done with regard to the culture and whether or not the right platforms are in place.

The lean omnichannel prioritization method

Let's for a moment assume that the future customer journey has been visualized and all necessary platforms have been established. Then the key question is: which parts of the customer journey are currently preventing you from achieving more profitable customer relationships? This prioritization is something you need to agree upon with your leading stakeholders with help from data analytics.

These parts of the customer journey are referred to as 'epics'. The term 'epic' is borrowed from the discipline of agile development and represents a body of work that is seen from an end user's (end customer's) perspective and can be broken down into more specific tasks – often referred to as 'user stories'. Each epic should be prioritized on high-level estimations of value versus effort.

Value in this case would incorporate:
- estimated short-term conversion benefits
- estimated long-term benefits in terms of customer lifetime value.

Effort would be the work needed to:
- build or adjust platform features
- create content and creative material
- orchestrate content, communicate, and automate marketing and CRM

- adjust training programmes and incentives to reflect new tasks
- train personnel in new tasks.

Prioritization should of course start with the epics that represent the lowest effort and the most value.

In line with the 'work hard, play hard' culture, it makes sense to look at your omnichannel customer journey in accordance with how Eric Ries defines the 'lean startup' – where, in this case, the new customer journey is your 'product'. In his 2011 book *The Lean Startup*, Ries advocates an iterative process of 'build, measure and learn' to enable companies to quickly progress and see what works and what doesn't.[59] In the context of introducing an omnichannel approach to an established business, given that you will start by leveraging existing knowledge and analysing existing data, you could argue that you'll mix Ries's approach up a bit and do 'learn, build, measure' instead.

The traditional 'build' phase of the lean startup approach entails more than coding on platforms. You need to distil the upcoming epics into what they mean for the platform teams, the marketing teams and the personnel servicing customers directly (in the customer service function and in-store). Which new features (the so-called user stories) do the platform teams need to develop in which order? What content do you need to develop and deploy? Who needs to perform which tasks in the future? How do you make sure they have the skills for that?

NEW SKILLS NEEDED – IN-HOUSE OR AGENCIES?

Having to build all omnichannel skills in-house is a major task for HR, regardless of whether it is done by hiring or by training current employees. Some competencies may temporarily require extra personnel while new platforms are established, with this demand decreasing once the operational phase is reached. For these projects, it makes sense to use the support of agencies and external system integrators to keep full time headcounts to a minimum. If however, you can afford a solid internal development department, this will provide you with a short time to market for initiatives and solutions because your developers know the existing solutions inside out.

Other specialized competencies will be needed, especially within analytics and to set up automated marketing. If you are in a relatively small organization, then consider whether it would be attainable to create a professional environment for each specific skill. Otherwise, you'll spend too much money acquiring a specialist who will quickly become lonely and uninspired and leave you before any real results have been created. If you can't create enough of a professional environment for any specific skills, then go for external support in that area instead of dedicated headcounts.

Tying it all together into a coherent customer experience

However tempting it may be to outsource parts of the production of omnichannel assets and platforms, make sure to build and retain enough skills to tie every single platform and initiative together into coherent customer experiences. The task of coordinating and prioritizing efforts should not be outsourced.

If you want to be a truly customer-centric company, then you cannot outsource customer-centricity.

This task is especially pertinent if you are working with multiple agencies on various channels and solutions. It requires a high degree of strategic overview and, not least, the project management to ensure that different solutions are integrated and that everyone is contributing positively to create a comprehensive customer experience. If you are working with a full-service agency, this coordinating governance function is less important. However, you will often buy specialized expertise for the individual channels. In all cases, the Omnichannel Hexagon can be a useful tool in this work.

MATURITY IN ORGANIZING & MANAGEMENT

Maturity within organizing and management can be summed as follows:

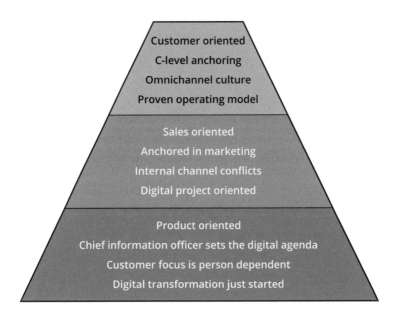

Highest maturity level

The mature omnichannel company has customer-centricity anchored with the CEO but with a dedicated direct report (such as the chief marketing officer, chief commercial officer or similar) centrally responsible for omnichannel customer experiences. Collaboration works well across departments. All functions understand their role, know what they must contribute and are motivated to actually do so through their incentive structures. Local markets are handled through a glocal approach that leverages both advantages of scale and localization. An omnichannel culture of putting the customer first permeates all departments and is sustained through a set omnichannel operating model and a focus on continuously building and maintaining omnichannel skills with respect to the most effective balance of insourcing versus outsourcing.

Middle maturity level

The organizations with average omnichannel maturity have a sales-oriented approach to the market. A true customer focus is solely found in marketing and sales, which run the customer-oriented projects with limited integration into the rest of the business. These companies often have a digital competence centre, where digital knowledge and competence is gathered. There is burgeoning collaboration between marketing and IT, but fundamental changes to the organizational and incentive structures remain to be made.

Lowest maturity level

The organizations that are working least maturely with omnichannel are mainly focused on optimizing their product on the basis of their own technological knowledge. A genuine customer focus depends on the initiatives of individual pioneers. Developmental measures are primarily about optimizing and scaling production in pace with sales, as well as maintaining the overall brand and image. The application of digital skills in relation to customers is limited and takes place with IT as a gatekeeper. IT is dedicated to ensuring the uptime and operation of business systems for manufacturing and sales and is not incentivized to help marketing.

Remember that you can take our test based on the Omnichannel Hexagon and find your company's omnichannel maturity level at:

OMNICHANNELFORBUSINESS.ORG

CONCLUSION

The most advanced organizations within omnichannel are the ones that are working consistently to build up a database of engaged customers whom they can recognize and communicate with in a proactive fashion across multiple channels. They have integrated customer data from multiple data sources, having submitted transactional, behavioural and emotional data for each individual customer, and they have made this data accessible to the marketing department through an integrated customer profile. They are continuously using AI and predictive analytics to gain insights from their customer data on both a macro and a customer level. Predictive models continuously determine the next best action for each individual customer, and these insights are directly coupled with the communicative actions and service that, along with the product, make up the customer experience. Communication and service leverage data for personalization whenever possible, and the organizations aim to create as many coherent and seamless customers journeys as they can, with as few resources as is feasible, through creative campaigns and automated communication across all channels. Omnichannel performance is evaluated through the use of customer metrics in order to secure the optimal creation of as many profitable customer relationships as possible. To make all of the above a reality, these organizations have organized themselves around omnichannel and thus aligned departmental structures and incentives towards being customer-centric.

Having read through the chapters of this book, you've probably given a lot of thought to how your company is doing in regard to each discipline. If you haven't done so already, we suggest you spend 20 minutes taking the survey in the omnichannel benchmark tool (see the links at the end of each chapter) to gain a deeper understanding of your maturity and how it compares to that of your competitors.

In the benchmark tool you can also find more detailed information on what you can do to progress further based on your specific responses and archetype. Does your organization resemble that of the archetypical Salesperson or perhaps more so the Scientist archetype? And what would the next best step be?

Unless you have only just started dipping your toes into working with omnichannel, the chances are that Organizing & Management is the discipline that is holding you back the most. That means you are at the point where you need help from other parts of the organization. Given omnichannel's all-encompassing nature, you cannot implement it alone. For the purpose of getting more people onboard, we can highly recommend inviting your colleagues to also fill out the survey in the benchmark tool and thus help get the conversation going and spread knowledge throughout your organization.

Once you are logged into the benchmark tool it's possible to obtain a personal link to share with your colleagues so that their responses become visible within the same account. That way you can both compare the joint result with the industry benchmark and can easily see where you agree or disagree internally.

What comes after omnichannel?

First we had multichannel, then cross-channel and now everybody is talking about omnichannel. To the untrained eye it may seem entirely like old wine in new bottles – the wine is more or less the same, but the label is different. So, what is next, you might ask? Will omnichannel survive as a concept?

The word 'omnichannel' has the benefit of being really hard to top. What's bigger than 'omni', after all? Nevertheless, the chances are that we won't be using the term 'omnichannel' ten years from now. But, even though it's hard to predict what the next label will be, we feel confident that it won't suddenly go out of fashion to communicate to customers with greater relevance and timeliness. Looking at it in this way makes it of less importance what label we decide to stick on the bottle.

We sincerely hope that you enjoyed reading this book and would be delighted to hear any feedback you might have from using the model and the benchmark tool.

Rasmus Houlind and Colin Shearer,
2019

ENDNOTES

1   Omnichannel-related technology at Nordstrom is often debated and referred to in online blogs related to e-commerce and digital marketing. See, for instance, Rachel Arthur, "Why Nordstrom's Latest Customer Experience Tool is all About Convenience" (Forbes), last modified 24 August 2017, https://www.forbes.com/sites/rachelarthur/2017/08/24/nordstrom-tech-customer-experience-convenience/#282d9134531d; Shea Marie Frates, "I Tried Nordstrom's Style Boards" (SheaMarieFrates), last modified 13 February 2018, https://www.sheamariefrates.com/i-tried-nordstroms-style-boards; Cameron Proffitt, "4 Perks of Nordstrom Curbside Pickup" (CameronProffitt), last modified 28 February 2018, https://www.cameronproffitt.com/nordstrom-curbside-pickup; and Stephan Serrano, "17 Omnichannel Strategies and Tactics Breakdown" (Barilliance), last modified 19 March 2018, https://www.barilliance.com/omnichannel-marketing-case-study.

2   "Nordstrom Investor Day 2018" (Nordstrom), accessed 21 January 2019, https://investor.nordstrom.com/events/event-details/nordstrom-investor-day-2018.

3   Emma Sopadjieva, Utpal M. Dholakia and Beth Benjamin, "A Study of 46,000 Shoppers Shows That Omnichannel Retailing Works" (Harvard Business Review), last modified 3 January 2017, https://hbr.org/2017/01/a-study-of-46000-shoppers-shows-that-omnichannel-retailing-works.

4   Mark Abraham, Steve Mitchelmore, Sean Collins et al., "Profiting from Personalization" (Boston Consulting Group), last modified 8 May 2017, https://www.bcg.com/publications/2017/retail-marketing-sales-profiting-personalization.aspx.

5   Mark Abraham, Steve Mitchelmore, Sean Collins et al., "Profiting from Personalization" (Boston Consulting Group), last modified 8 May 2017, https://www.bcg.com/publications/2017/retail-marketing-sales-profiting-personalization.aspx.

6   Mark Hook, "Study: 87% of Retailers Agree Omnichannel Is Critical to Their Business, Yet Only 8% Have 'Mastered' It" (Brightpearl), last modified 15 December 2017, https://www.brightpearl.com/company/press-and-media-1/2017/12/15/study-87-of-retailers-agree-omnichannel-is-critical-to-their-business-yet-only-8-have-mastered-it.

7   Jim Blasingame, "It's the Age of the Customer – Are You Ready?" (Forbes), last modified 27 January 2014, https://www.forbes.com/sites/jimblasingame/2014/01/27/its-the-age-of-the-customer-are-you-ready/#635d1428119a.

8   Simon Eaves, Sohel Aziz, Larry Thomas, Søren Kristensen and Shantel Moses, *Marketing in the New* (Accenture, 2016), accessed 19 January 2019, https://www.accenture.com/us-en/_acnmedia/Accenture/next-gen-4/future-of-marketing/Accenture-Marketing-In-The-New-January-2017.pdf.

9   Don Peppers and Martha Rogers, *The One-to-One Future* (London: Piatkus, 1993).

10 Jim Blasingame, *The Age of the Customer* (SBN Books, 2014).

11 Read more about paid, owned and earned media in Chapter 4.

12 Inspiration and confirmed approval through direct conversations with customer relationship manager Harlen Xing from Forevermark.

13 See for instance Alf Jondahl from the Norwegian retailer VITA's presentation from Agillic Summit 2018: https://vimeo.com/274392959 go to 16:09

14 "2017 Q4 Quarterly Report" (Nordstrom, 2017), accessed 21 January 2019, https://press.nordstrom.com/financial-information/quarterly-results.

15 Tony Fontana, "DSW's Omnichannel Transformation" (National Retail Federation), last modified 10 August 2016, https://nrf.com/blog/dsws-omnichannel-transformation.

16 See, for instance, www.utopia.ai.

17 Associated Press, "Check-In with Facial Recognition Now Possible in Shanghai" (VOA News), last modified 16 October 2018, https://www.voanews.com/a/check-in-with-facial-recognition-now-possible-in-shanghai/4615792.html.

18 Bien Perez, "Shanghai Metro Gets Tech Upgrade from Alibaba" (South China Morning Post), last modified 6 December 2017, https://www.scmp.com/tech/enterprises/article/2123014/shanghai-subway-use-alibaba-voice-and-facial-recognition-systems-ai.

19 OMD and Insights Group, OMDReview, March 2014, not publicly available, Claus Andersen from OMD quotes the study in an article on the Danish Marketing Association's website: Christian W. Larsen, Den Dag Aida Døde, https://markedsforing.dk/artikler/pr-kommunikation/den-dag-aida-d-de, Markedsføring.dk, 16 January 2014. Accessed January 2019.

20 *Response Rate 2012 Report* (DMA, 2012), accessed 19 January 2019, http://www.marketingedge.org/sites/default/files/ProfessorsAcademy/2012-Response-Rate-Report-(Final).pdf.

21 For instance, through the company Experian. See www.experian.com.

22 COMAPI (previously Dynmark) claims a 98% open rate for text messages, with 90% being read within the first three seconds. See *Big Data: Profiling Your Customers, Mobile Intelligence Review – Edition 2* (COMAPI, 2014).

23 "2017 Q4 Quarterly Report" (Nordstrom, 2017), accessed 21 January 2019, https://press.nordstrom.com/financial-information/quarterly-results.

24 See http://Nordstrom.com.

25 Barb Darrow, "LinkedIn Claims Half a Billion Users" (Fortune), last modified 24 April 2017, http://fortune.com/2017/04/24/linkedin-users.

26 "Nike Privacy Policy" (Nike), last modified 18 May 2018, https://swoo.sh/2pOfhb8.

27 Nicole Giannopoulos, "Burberry Drives Revenue and Loyalty with iPads" (RISNews), last modified 18 November 2013, https://risnews.com/burberry-drives-revenue-and-loyalty-ipads.

28 "Case Study: Cablecom Reduces Churn with the Help of Predictive Analytics" (tdwi), last modified 18 October 2007, https://tdwi.org/articles/2007/10/18/case-study-cablecom-reduces-churn-with-the-help-of-predictive-analytics.aspx.

29 Thomas H. Davenport and D. J. Patil, "Data Scientist: The Sexiest Job of the 21st Century" (Harvard Business Review), last modified October 2012, https://hbr.org/2012/10/data-scientist-the-sexiest-job-of-the-21st-century.

30 "Banco Itaú Argentina: Optimizing Customer Cross-Selling and Acquisition Strategies with Predictive Analytics" (IBM), last modified 18 November 2010, https://www-07.ibm.com/sg/clientstories/cases/banco_itau_argentina.html?id.

31 See http://www.thenorthface.com/xps.

32 See Laura Beaudin and Francine Gierak, *It's About Time: Why Your Marketing May Be Falling Short* (Bain & Company, 2018) accessed 19 January 2019, https://services.google.com/fh/files/misc/report-bain-marketing.pdf.

33 David Moth, "15 Stats That Show Why Click-And-Collect Is So Important For Retailers" (econsultancy), last modified 18 November 2013, https://econsultancy.com/15-stats-that-show-why-click-and-collect-is-so-important-for-retailers.

34 Joe Keenan (interviewer), "Inside Suitsupply's Omnichannel Approach" (Total Retail) accessed 19 January 2019, https://www.mytotalretail.com/video/single/inside-suitsupplys-omnichannel-approach.

35 Greta J, "Amazon AI Designed to Create Phone Cases Terribly Malfunctions" (BoredPanda), accessed 19 January 2019, https://www.boredpanda.com/funny-amazon-ai-designed-phone-cases-fail.

36 Sophia Bernazzani, "The Decline of Organic Facebook Reach & How to Adjust to the Algorithm" (Hubspot) last modified 3 May 2018, https://blog.hubspot.com/marketing/facebook-organic-reach-declining. In this article Bernazzani references multiple studies, including two from 2014 citing rates as low as 6.5% and even 2%. According to Bernazzani, organic reach has gone down even further since then.

37 Samuel M. McClure, Jian Li, Damon Tomlin, Kim S. Cypert, Latané M. Montague and P. Read Montague, "Neural Correlates of Behavioral Preference for Culturally Familiar Drinks," *Neuron* 44 (2004): 379-387.

38 Daniel Kahneman, *Thinking, Fast and Slow* (London: Allen Lane, 2011).

39 Stuart Lauchlan, "The Integration Imperative at Nordstrom – Striking the Omni-Channel Balance" (Diginomica), last modified 5 March 2018, https://diginomica.com/2018/03/05/integration-imperative-nordstrom-striking-omni-channel-balance; "Nordstrom (JWN) Q4 2017 Results – Earnings Call Transcript" (SeekingAlpha), last modified 1 March 2018, https://seekingalpha.com/article/4152608-nordstrom-jwn-q4-2017-results-earnings-call-transcript?part=single.

40 Paul W. Farris, Neil T. Bendle, Phillip E. Pfeifer and David J. Reibstein, *Marketing Metrics* (US: Pearson Education, 2015).

41 Fred Reichheld, *The Ultimate Question* (Boston: Harvard Business School Publishing, 2006).

42 "Customer Lifetime Value to Customer Acquisition Ratio (CLV:CAC)" (Klipfolio), accessed 19 January 2019, https://www.klipfolio.com/resources/kpi-examples/saas-metrics/customer-lifetime-value-to-customer-acquisition-ratio.

43 In the Nordstrom report, sales per square foot is referred to as 'comps pr square foot'. "Nordstrom Inc. 2017 Q4 - Results - Earnings Call Slides" (SeekingAlpha), last modified 25 February 2018, https://seekingalpha.com/article/4152607-nordstrom-inc-2017-q4-results-earnings-call-slides.

44 See for instance: https://www.marketingteacher.com/boston-matrix/

45 Fred Reichheld, *The Ultimate Question* (Boston: Harvard Business School Publishing, 2006).

46 Inspiration from Brian Honigman, "How Sephora Integrates Retail & Digital Marketing" (WBR Insights), last modified 27 June 2018, https://etailwest.wbre-search.com/how-sephora-integrates-retail-online-marketing; Sephora Teardown, "How Sephora Built a Beauty Empire to Survive the Retail Apocalypse" (CB Insights), accessed 19 January 2019, https://www.cbinsights.com/research/report/sephora-teardown; "Sephora Visual Artist – Powered by ModiFace" (Vimeo), last modified 2018, https://vimeo.com/220504292; and "We Are Sephora" (Sephora Employee Community Site), accessed 25 January 2019, www.wearesephora.com.

47 John P. Kotter, *Leading Change* (Boston, MA: Harvard Business Publishing, 2012).

48 *Rethink the Role of the CMO* (Forrester, 2018), accessed 19 January 2019, https://www.accenture.com/t20181002T182512Z__w__/us-en/_acnmedia/PDF-87/Accenture-Rethink-the-role-of-the-CMO.pdf.

49 Mark Abraham, Steve Mitchelmore, Sean Collins, Jeff Maness, Mark Kistulinec, Shervin Khodabandeh, Daniel Hoenig and Jody Visse, "Profiting from Personalization" (Boston Consulting Group), last modified 8 May 2017, https://www.bcg.com/publications/2017/retail-marketing-sales-profiting-personalization.aspx.

50 Hilary Milnes, "Why Sephora Merged Its Digital and Physical Retail Teams into One Department" (Glossy), last modified 6 April 2018, https://www.glossy.co/new-face-of-beauty/why-sephora-merged-its-digital-and-physical-retail-teams-into-one-department.

51 Emma Sopadjieva, Utpal M. Dholakia and Beth Benjamin, "A Study of 46,000 Shoppers Shows that Omnichannel Retailing Works" (Harvard Business Review), last modified 3 January 2017, https://hbr.org/2017/01/a-study-of-46000-shoppers-shows-that-omnichannel-retailing-works.

52 JDA and Centiro, *JDA & Centiro Customer Pulse 2017: European Comparison* (JDA, 2017), accessed 19 January 2019, http://now.jda.com/rs/366-TWM-779/images/Customer%20Pulse%202017%20European%20Comparison.pdf.

53 Herbert Lui, "10 Best Omni-Channel Retailers and What You Can Learn from Them" (Shopify), last modified 11 August 2017, https://www.shopify.com/enterprise/10-best-omni-channel-retailers-and-what-you-can-learn-from-them.

54 Homa Zaryouni, "Williams Sonoma: A 20-Year Head Start in Omnichannel" (GartnerL2), last modified 7 July 2015, https://www.l2inc.com/daily-insights/williams-sonoma-a-20-year-head-start-in-omnichannel.

55 Terrence E. Deal and Allan A. Kennedy, *Corporate Cultures* (Cambridge: Perseus, 2000).

56 Ruth Umoh, "Jeff Bezos: When You Find A Business Opportunity With These Traits, 'Don't Just Swipe Right, Get Married'" (CNBC), last modified 14 September 2018, https://www.cnbc.com/2018/09/13/amazon-jeff-bezos-4-traits-a-good-business-opportunity-should-have.html.

57 Terrence E. Deal and Allan A. Kennedy, *Corporate Cultures* (Cambridge: Perseus, 2000).

58 See www.wearesephora.com.

59 Eric Ries, *The Lean Startup* (London: Portfolio Penguin, 2011).

ACKNOWLEDGMENTS

The famous scientist Alfred Newton once said: "If I have seen further it is only because I'm standing on the shoulders of giants". This same can indeed be said about this book. By no means can we, the authors, take full credit for the making of this book and the omnichannel hexagon. So many helpful and inspiring people have played a big part in making the framework and the book come to life that we feel the need to show our gratitude and do our acknowledgements. It is indeed different people who know the inner workings of organizational incentive models and artificial intelligence. Without you all, this book and the Omnichannel Hexagon would never have been as bullet proof as we like to believe it is.

First of all, we'd like to thank the approximately 60 people who took part of the research process for the first version of *Make It All About Me* a few years back. You know who you are – thanks again! The readers of the first version also deserve a big shout out – thanks for reading, commenting, discussing and booking talks, keynotes and workshops and thank you for using the omnichannel benchmark tool in your theses, businesses and with your clients.

Second, thanks to all the new people who helped sharpen and update the omnichannel hexagon to an international enterprise mindset. Ian Dewar from The North Face, Arek Zakonek and Berend Sikkenga from LEGO, Harlen Xing from Forevermark, Justin Sandee from bol.com, Martin Jonassen from Storytel, Monique Elliot from AAB Electric, Matthew Brown from EchoChamber.com, Stefan Kirkedal from Matas, Mattias Andersson from House of Friends, Rasmus Riddersholm from Telenor (now Ørsted), Arild Horsberg from Netlife, Peter Schlegel from Responsive, author Christina Bouttrup, Zvi Goldstein from Interflora, Puni Rajah from Governance Reviews and Gunjan Bhow from Disney.

We'd also like to thank the team from the Networked Business Initiative – especially CEO Jan Futtrup Kjær for the long-lasting collaboration on the omnichannel benchmark tool. Thanks for seeing the potential and making it come to life together with the Chamber of Commerce in Copenhagen. Thanks to Carsten Johansen from Networked Business Initiative for being a rock-solid pillar in the update of the questionnaire framework, turning it into an even more helpful tool for organizations around the world.

Also, a big thank you to our colleagues in the marketing technology company Agillic and the data scientists from Houston Analytics. Jesper Valentin Holm, Bo Sannung, Thomas Gaarde Andersen, Antti Syväniemi and all the rest – thanks for sparring and helping develop a deeper understanding of omnichannel and analytics and for covering for us when we were covered in omnichannel mud and couldn't help seeing rainbow colored hexagons everywhere.

Our publishers deserve a thank you as well – Niki Mullin for having the patience waiting for us getting ready to write, Sara Taheri, Susan Furber and Hazel Bird for thorough editing and kind criticism. You all helped make the book sharper and more to the point.

Last but not least – our families, wives and kids, for showing great patience when we weren't (even just mentally) present to be the husbands and fathers that we'd like to be.

ABOUT THE AUTHORS

Rasmus Houlind is a thought leader within omnichannel and digital marketing. Through more than a decade with major Scandinavian agencies, he's worked with some of the largest brands in the Nordics. His work as a consultant and an author has helped him to build his knowledge of marketing and CRM. Since 2015, he's been Chief Strategy Officer with the marketing technology company, Agillic.

Colin Shearer has been a pioneer and thought leader in AI and advanced analytics for over 25 years. His experience ranges from successful start-ups and the creation of market-leading tools and technology – he designed and developed the Clementine Data mining System, now IBM SPSS Modeler – to worldwide executive roles with the largest vendors. In December 2016, Colin joined Houston Analytics, a Finland-based European leader in artificial intelligence, to become Chief Strategy Officer.